D11166639

5 GIFTS *for an Abundant Life*

5 Gifts for an Abundant Life

Create a Consciousness
of Wealth

DIANE HARMONY

UNIVERSAL HARMONY HOUSE
Del Mar, California

Universal Harmony House
2658 Del Mar Heights Road #199
Del Mar, CA 92014
www.5GIFTS.com

Revised, June, 2007

Edited by: Mo Rafael
Cover and interior design: Suzanne Albertson

Harmony, Diane 1942–
    5 gifts for an abundant life : creating a consciousness of wealth /
Diane Harmony —1st ed.—Del Mar, Calif. : Universal Harmony, 2004.
    p.   cm.
    ISBN: 978-0-9742749-0-4
    1. Self-actualization (Psychology)—Religious aspects. 2. Success—Religious aspects. 3. Spiritual life. 4. Spirituality. I. Title. II. Five gifts for an abundant life.

BF637.S4 H37 2004   2003096407
158.1—dc22   0401

*This book is dedicated to my source of boundless
abundant life, my grandchildren
Melissa, J and Ella Grace*

*and in memory of
Rev. Margaret Wright*

My Thanks

*I*t takes a tribe to write a book. The prayers, encouragement, technical contributions, love and emotional upliftment of so many angels visibly and invisibly guided each step along the path to the fulfillment of this vision.

My deepest GIFT of Gratitude is given to my dear friend and associate, Vivianne Thomas, for her precious friendship, unwavering vision, unconditional commitment and dedication to *5 GIFTS for an Abundant Life* as a course and as a book. I give thanks to my editor, Mo Rafael, for her clarity, coaching and brilliant wordsmith work that is found on each page. To my daughter Shannon Geisbert, for her beautiful presence and complete willingness to carry out a myriad of communication tasks, for her cheerleading and for the public relations brilliance she has brought to this Divine Idea, I am forever grateful.

My deepest thanks go to the email prayer circle of women friends who gave the gift of weekly prayer for this project: Karen Axnick, Rev. Dr. Sage Bennet, Tina Fox, Mo Rafael, Michelle Spieker, Joan Thornton, Michelle Tiernan, Vivianne Thomas, and Rev. Margaret Wright. And to those dear, blessed souls who reviewed the manuscript and shared their wisdom: my children Shannon, Dr. Mindy Nagle, Polly Peterson, and John and Lisa Nagle, my sister, Gail Gulliksen, my editing friend Sheri Penney, Rev. Dr. Michael Beckwith, Rev. Dr. Christian Sorensen, Gena Garrett Momyer, Karen Pitt, Tina Fox, Peggy Reynolds, Rev. Margaret Wright . . . *Thank You!*

To the students and Certified Facilitators of the *5 GIFTS for an Abundant Life*™ course that is offered around the country, my gratitude for living these GIFTS and, through your own transformations of consciousness, validating the worth of this work.

My gratitude to the wonderful Vision Core of Universal Harmony Inc. that is continually allowing God's idea of this work to be revealed through them: Kevin Finneran, Shannon Geisbert, Carolyn and Ray Holder, Elaine Lyttleton, Mollie Malone, Dianne McCourtney, Karin O'Mahony, Mo Rafael, Jed Staley, Vivianne Thomas and Paul Lloyd Warner.

And finally, thank you Suzanne Albertson for bringing this book to life.

Contents

Foreword

In 1976 I made a commitment to the lord of my being, the goddess within me, that I would be 100% responsible for the transformation of the abundance consciousness of Planet Earth.

For all the years since, I have been a student and a teacher of the spiritual laws of abundance, the spiritual principles that govern our demonstration of the never-failing, infinite supply to meet every need and every desire. I have proven in my own life that there are powerful gifts available to each of us and all we have to do is claim them. For this I am eternally thankful.

We have had great and powerful teachers. I am particularly grateful for Charles and Myrtle Fillmore, Ernest Holmes, Catherine Ponder, John Rankin, Sig Paulsen, Paula McClellan, Harriet Vallier, John Randolph and Jan Price, and now . . . DIANE HARMONY.

In 5 GIFTS for an Abundant Life, Diane gives us all a very special gift. She offers us a fresh and vibrant way to look at time-honored prosperity principles. She helps us to see with new eyes, to act with a deeper understanding. It is an honor to have been asked to write this Foreword.

So here it is. . .

My prayer is that you will be good to yourself, that you will devour the information Diane Harmony presents so carefully and so lovingly.

Your job is to take action, to get up out of your comfort zone and follow her suggestions. I invite you to read this as a workbook, and to prayerfully and with great expectancy of good, do your part.

May you open your 5 GIFTS and celebrate the life you desire and deserve, with a sense of awe and wonder of the graciousness of universal love.

Your future is absolutely in your hands in this wonderful instruction manual. You have loved yourself enough to open the pages, so we know you have what it takes to follow through, always being consciously appreciative for the author's understanding and her generosity in sharing it with us all.

Richest Blessing,

Edwene Gaines

Owner-director,
Rock Ridge Retreat Center
Unity Minister
Director, The Masters' School

Preface

e live in a Finished Kingdom. All that we could possibly want, need or desire is already in form . . . or in an idea that would create it. We have been told through the ages, "It is God's good pleasure to give us the Kingdom." We live in a friendly universe that is designed to support us. We are the direct descendants of the Infinite Source of All Good.

There is a place inside of you and me where this truth is alive and well. This place is the home of our Divine Nature. It is the source of our longing to experience a life of prosperity, affluence and fulfillment. This yearning is far more than an ego directive to be happy and successful in the world—although we usually are happy when living an Abundant Life. I believe it is a true *calling* by the God Presence within us to more completely express the truth of our being. This book is my invitation to you to let yourself feel that deep yearning from within to live fully expressed, fully supported by good health, abundant finances, rewarding and wholesome relationships, and abounding opportunities to give your unique gifts to others.

The 5 GIFTS I am sharing with you are based on the wisdom I have gleaned from the Divine Power I call God, the God that is within me and within you. You may not believe in God or even a Higher Power, or perhaps the God you know lives separate from you in the heavens, the animals, the plants or the seasons. Your God may have a different name . . . Spirit, Divine Intelligence, Intuition, Life, Sacred Heart, Allah, Mana, Krishna, or something else. When I use the term *God* I am referring to the Invisible Spirit that takes great pleasure in "giving us the Kingdom." (Please read these pages using whatever name you wish for the One Source.)

If we were to recognize that God is Whole, Perfect and Complete, it would be impossible to attribute any idea of lack, limitation, disease, pain or poverty to Spirit. If we were to further recognize that we are divine expressions of God, we could also deduce that we would be out of alignment with our spiritual natures if we entertain any ideas of lack or limitation.

I suggest we do recognize and fully accept these premises, realizing that it is our very nature to *be* the Abundance of God. (To be the Abundance of God means to believe in, to trust, to express and to know ourselves *as* the Abundance of God.)

When we agree to the premise that we are expressions of God's Abundance, what do we do with the old beliefs we have put our faith in up until now? What *can* we do with those beliefs that have repeatedly demonstrated themselves in our lives as experiences of "less than enough": financial hardship (money), illness (health), co-dependent and unsatisfactory relationships (love of self and others), and unfulfilling jobs that just pay the bills (fulfillment in careers that showcase our gifts and talents), to name a few.

We simply let them go. Knowing that we have tried every which way to "make them work," we finally allow ourselves to let go of them. We release all of those limiting ideas and beliefs with love. And we release them with gratitude for the ways in which they have served us, both consciously and unconsciously, up until now. By releasing our limiting beliefs we reclaim the power they have had over our lives. We free ourselves from *the illusion of not enough*.

The process of freeing ourselves from this illusion has all the elements of an adventurous journey. This book is a guide for that journey—from these limiting beliefs into a consciousness of wealth. It is the greatest journey life has to offer because of the transformational gifts we receive along the way. There are five of them . . . hence the title of this book, 5 GIFTS *for an Abundant Life*.

The word *GIFTS* is an acronym for the five principles we encounter on our journey: Gratitude, Intentions, Forgiveness, Tithing and Surrender. I call them *GIFTS* because these spiritual principles open us to an awareness of the abundance that is our Divine Nature. When we receive the 5 GIFTS we move from our limited mental understanding (*in the mind of our minds*) of these rich spiritual principles to a full acceptance and intuitive knowing of them (*in the Mind of our Hearts*). At one and the same time, that journey from head to heart is the shortest and the most fantastic journey of our lives. By shifting our focal point from the mind of the mind (the rational thinker) to the Mind of the Heart (our intuitive Knower), we are re-routing our perception of everything, including our definitions of ourselves. This journey moves us from lack thinking to abundance knowing, from apparent separation from our Source to acceptance of our divine destiny *as* God's living revelation of infinite supply and unconditional love.

Gratitude . . . Intentions . . . Forgiveness . . . Tithing . . . Surrender. Why these particular GIFTS? Because each of these GIFTS has been carefully "test driven" for the power to shift consciousness. The ancient and modern mystics alike, no matter what their root tradition, have consistently named these five principles as essential disciplines of any spiritual practice. We can use these spiritual principles to *change our beliefs* and, as a direct result, we will change the experiences in our lives.

We have the power as spiritual beings to transmute the appearances of the conditions we see about us. In other words, we can use our inner eyes and ears to see and hear beyond what is delivered by our five senses. But how do we access these inner senses? By putting the 5 GIFTS into practice—that is, by receiving and giving them.

Gratitude, Intentions, Forgiveness, Tithing and Surrender have the power to transform our experience of life, allowing us to consciously connect with the vast invisible realm that lies beyond the finite, "sense-able" world. These 5 GIFTS enable us (without denying, minimizing or overriding any of the facts of our three-dimensional reality) to embrace the multidimensional Reality of Life. In this Reality we are not distracted by the "appearances" of the human condition. In this consciousness we are immersed in Divine Wisdom and we know who we truly are. We are Spirit . . . Love, Beauty, Harmony, Joy, Abundance, Peace.

The time is at hand for us to make this leap of consciousness from lives run by self-limiting beliefs based on sensory information to lives run by our souls' vision of what is possible. It is time to make the journey from the mind of the mind to the Mind of the Heart. Our destination, which we will discover to be our greatest joy, is to know that we are already living in the Finished Kingdom.

My intention is to empower you to receive and accept the 5 GIFTS as the vehicle for your journey. I invite you to release any idea that your journey has to be hard or that you're not strong enough, smart enough, young enough, old enough, enlightened enough or good enough to begin. If you, instead, live in the expectancy that this transformational trip is going to be fun and joy-filled . . . what a gift you will be giving to yourself!

With Abundant Blessings,

Diane Harmony

P.S.   I want to share with you a few insights about particular words, phrases and metaphors that I have used throughout this book. The first is that I have used the words "apparently," "apparent," "appearance," and "appear" in their most literal sense—one that we often overlook. According to Webster's Collegiate

Dictionary Tenth Edition, *appearance* means "external show, semblance, outward aspect." It is my intention in this book to assist you to open your awareness to the extreme limitation of our finite world of appearances, because we are, in truth, beings of infinite possibilities. We are so much more than our sensory, *do-ing* selves. We are human *be-ings* endowed with enormous spiritual power to transcend the appearances delivered by our five senses.

Second, you will find that I use all forms of the verb "(to) name" throughout this book. The idea of "naming" or labeling a thing is unique to our species. As we use this privilege, we speak (or think) words of enormous power. For example, when we call something good or bad, possible or impossible, inspiration or damnation, heaven or hell, we unleash beliefs inherent in that name that fulfill themselves. Without being aware of it, we are opening Genie's bottle every time we put a name on someone or something. In addressing this powerful tool of *naming* in the following pages, my intention is for you to realize that you have the opportunity to harness the power of this tool consciously, so that it can work for your highest good.

Third, when I refer to any of the 5 GIFTS for an Abundant Life they will be written in all capital letters, e.g., GRATITUDE. I want them to appear bigger than life because they have the potential to expand our lives in such profound ways!

Finally, I have tried to draw clear distinctions between our old, three-dimensional ways of thinking and multidimensional, soul consciousness. One of the ways I make reference to these distinctions is by the terms "mind of the mind" (or "mind of our minds") and *Mind of the Heart (or Mind of our Hearts)*, respectively. Another way that I have delineated them is by placing key words or terms, when I first introduce them, in quotation marks or italics. I have used quotation marks to help set off words and phrases that denote or come from old, three-dimensional patterns of thought (as in "mind of the mind," above) and italics to bring our attention to deeper meanings and expanded modes of thought (as in *Mind of the Heart*, above).

INTRODUCTION

Our Journey Begins

Welcome to a journey of awakening . . . the awakening of your power to live an Abundant Life. You are about to embark on an exploration of your own inexhaustible Inner Resources which are so much greater than what is *apparently* available to you in your present life!

Preparing for the Journey

For this journey you won't need the usual things that one takes on a big trip—passports, clothes for several different weather conditions, toiletries, money and exchange rate cards. No, on this excursion all you'll need is a willing mind and an open heart. "Willing and open for what," you ask? Willing to let go of the mental patterns of beliefs and the behaviors that have resulted in your living a life that is less than what you have always wanted. And willing to open your heart to embrace new ideas and new practices that will truly result in the ability to manifest your deepest desires. While my primary intention in guiding you on this adventure is not the creation of health, wealth, career and relationship success in your life, I believe that all these and so much more shall be yours. Rather, my first intention is to hold the space for you to become fully liberated from all survival fears so that you are free to devote your time, resources and energies to deepening your connection with your Infinite Source and living more of your Divine Self . . . to the fullest possibility of who you are.

Baggage to Leave Behind

Many of us have struggled with some aspect of lack in our lives—not enough time, opportunities, food, well-being, quality relationships, education, money, friends, and so on. Whether we realize it or not, we have been using the "pain" of those *apparent* conditions as a very powerful teacher so that we may learn to know Oneness in God. Rather than allowing *Vision* to pull us into awareness of how beautiful, powerful, wonderful and holy we are, we have chosen to be pushed into that awareness through pain, believing that we are separate from the Infinite Source of all. Exquisitely tormented by the pain of not enough love, time, money and/or health, we have been forced to resort to one or more of the following human solutions to our suffering:

- We create addictions to work, drugs, food, alcohol, or sex to numb the pain.
- We live lives of quiet desperation, feeling like this condition must be the punishment we deserve for being such bad people, and hoping that by some miracle it will all go away.
- We grope for yet one more solution we can impose that will "fix" the situation or make it better, such as changing jobs, trying one more health cure or divorcing our mate.

Eventually, we will have exhausted any number of these methods and hit our wall. Feeling utterly defeated, we will know that the jig is up when we can't haul our accumulated baggage forward one more step. Down on all fours under the unbearable weight of our "teacher," pain, we can do nothing but wave the white flag of truce and yell into the void, "I give up!" The end has finally come and we have no recourse but to *Let Go and Let God*. What an overwhelming time this is.

And what an enormously powerful time! Yes, powerful. Because it is only when our ego minds have run out of temporary solutions, avoidance patterns and rationalizations that the Mind of our Hearts can open to the Grace of God. Always there and waiting for an invitation from us, the Grace of God, *the ever-present, unconditional giving of God to Its creation,* is truly the answer to our prayers and beseechings. When we embrace the Grace of God we are no longer forced to learn our life lessons at the mercy of pain. Instead, we are open to living life guided by *Vision* and *Inspiration.* As one of my mentors taught me at a critical crossroad in my journey, "When you have nowhere else to turn, you are teachable."

From the Low Road to the High Road: My Personal Journey

I used to be a professional student at the School of Pain. For well over 40 years I believed that I was a helpless victim of my life circumstances demonstrating as a lack of money. I was certain that I was being punished for untold sins, as I struggled to "make it" in the world. Pain became the professor in my chosen survival major—Finances. Convinced that I was helpless to solve the never-ending problem of too little salary and too many bills, I felt entirely justified in blaming my situation on all sorts of scapegoats. I claimed that I was a victim of the economy, my marital status, my sex, my education, my boss, my God (who had surely forsaken me). I held the belief that the number of dollars in my checking account defined my self-worth.

You can imagine how low my self-esteem fell during the financial ebbs of my life, such as the time when the ATM would not allow a withdrawal because my balance had fallen below $20! I also believed that all the dollars I did receive had to be earned by the sweat of my brow and that it was my lot in life to never have

5

enough money. I just knew that life was meant to be a struggle, and then you died!

As I matriculated through the School of Pain I finally came to one accelerated course that had life-changing effects. A few years ago I found myself at the wedding celebration of my precious daughter with not a single dime to pay my way, much less contribute to her special day. Having to tell her and her wonderful husband-to-be that I had to renege on my promise to contribute to their marriage day took me down to all fours. "Oh my God," I thought, "could I get any lower than this?" The shame and guilt I felt over earlier debt I had incurred, the bankruptcy I had declared seven years before, and the begging I had done from friends just to pay the rent all paled in comparison to the utter hopelessness and despair I felt on this occasion of the happiest day of my daughter's life.

I cried oceans of tears into the wee hours of that wedding day morning. "How have I gotten myself into this pathetic place? I've worked so hard, raised three kids as a single mom and been a religious person—what did ever I do to deserve this? What am I missing?" I spent the pre-dawn hours of that day submerging myself in my familiar victim mode of self-blame and self-flagellation. At one point in this vicious downward spiral, in a space between the tears, I heard a soft voice say, "Be Still." Startled, I obeyed and stopped my sobbing. "What are you grateful for *right now*?" the Voice quietly asked. "That I'm breathing" is all I could answer. I felt the tiniest measure of calm inch its way through my shuddering body. "Will you surrender all your problems to Me?" the Voice asked. "And will you trust Me?" It gently inquired. "I have no choice," I sighed. "I have nowhere else to go. I have tried every way I know to fix this endless financial mess. All I want to do right now is to enjoy being the mother of the bride," I declared, feeling a little bit less hysterical. "Continue to be grateful and watch the miracles unfold today. Turn it all over to Me and have a wonderful time," the Voice said. "When you are grateful you open the door for My Abundance to flow into your life."

That fateful, extraordinary day I summarily transferred from the School of Pain to the School of Vision. Little did I realize how easy it is to be accepted at this school and how welcoming it feels. I received so much support from others there that I never felt like "the new kid on the block." And what a surprise it was to find everyone around me expressing their gratitude that I had made the decision to join them.

Attending this school guarantees every student a degree in listening with the inner ear to the Divine Plan for one's life. Here we are taught through inspiration, intuition and imagination what our true purpose is. Here we learn to choose the high road to clarity. And here we hone the skills needed to express that clarity. By the time we graduate from the School of Vision we have recognized that the Universe is *for* us and that It truly works *for* our highest good. The diploma we receive certifies our knowledge that *in God all things are possible.*

In the School of Vision my teachers have been many and my path one of joy and harmony, with only a few stumbles along the way. Through this new curriculum I have learned that what I was getting in life was determined by what I was giving. As I gave out fear and the belief that there was not enough, so was I receiving—with predictable mirroring—a life experience of fear and lack. It slowly dawned on me that I was using the Law of Giving and Receiving, "As you give, so shall you receive," in ways that actually kept the cycle of lack going in my life. The many profound classes I have taken in the School of Vision have taught me to *give out* everything that I want returned to me, including money, laughter, healthy choices, love, compassion, peace and harmony.

AS YOU GIVE, SO SHALL YOU RECEIVE.

... The Happy Ending

It was on a cloud of profound GRATITUDE that I floated into the bride's dressing room on my daughter's wedding day—gratitude for the bride, my son-in-love to be, my two ex-husbands who were attending to last minute details, the sprays of beautiful flowers and corsages that had just been delivered, and the flush of excitement on my other children's faces. Everywhere I looked I said, "Thank You, God!" God's floodgates opened, the miracles poured forth and I received. Money was slipped into my hand by a wise and generous sister to pay for my hotel room. "Thank you, God!" An offer to buy my breakfast came from my loving son from across the table of ten. "Thank you, God!" An idea for the perfect gift to give the newlyweds that cost my time and my talent, yet would be priceless to them, suddenly occurred to me. "Thank you, God!" A request for my counseling services came from a guest among the crowd of friends and family at the reception. "Thank you, God!" And as I gave each prayer of GRATITUDE, I received even more from the Infinite One Source, God.

And Here is Where Your Journey Begins

GRATITUDE, the first of the 5 GIFTS, is the GIFT that catapulted me ahead on my journey. With joy overflowing in my heart, I want to acknowledge you for accepting your soul's invitation to begin your journey of awakening. Wherever you may be along your path, I invite you to see this moment as the defining crossroads that it is. For I know the transforming power of the path of the 5 GIFTS that lies just ahead of you! By choosing this new path you are allowing these 5 GIFTS to lighten your load, sweeten your every step, light up your life and transform your consciousness. And I know that the Divine Power that revealed them to me is the very same Power that is within you.

For there is only One Source of our Good—be that Good a healthy and vibrant body; enough money to meet our every desire; rich, wholesome and loving relationships; or a rewarding career that utilizes all of the unique gifts we are here to give our fellow beings and the planet. The delivery systems of our good may be many, but there is only One Source: God. Sharing the gateways that open the channels to that Source is the purpose of 5 GIFTS *for an Abundant Life*. By giving these GIFTS you shall receive.

Travel Tips

Before going on to the next chapter, please allow yourself ten minutes of quiet time in which to read, absorb and commit yourself to the information that comes next. The following guidelines will assist you, as they have my students, in receiving **all** that the 5 GIFTS have to give you. Allow yourself the gift of playing some soft music, such as Peter Kater's "Compassion" or "Shamanic Dream" by Anugama, to set the tone for opening your heart and clearing your mind. Maybe you'd like to take your music and yourself to a place in nature where you feel in communion with Presence of Spirit. Just pamper yourself a little bit, in order to create a safe and loving environment for you to align yourself with these requests.

1. Choose a Prosperity Prayer Partner. The work of giving and receiving the 5 GIFTS is meant to be shared. Take a moment to become still and ask to be guided to identify the perfect person with whom to take this journey. Once that soul brother or sister has come into your awareness, plan to give them a copy of this book, and ask them to join you on this road to transformation. Make an agreement between you to read this book together and vow to support each other with weekly prayer. Also, be sure to

commit with your partner to take the time to do the exercises at the end of each of the GIFT chapters.

2. Give yourself the gifts of peace and comfort that come from a daily practice of meditation and prayer. Resolve to take thirty minutes each day for these essential spiritual practices while reading this book and doing the suggested exercises. (See the Appendix for prayer and meditation guidelines as well as suggested reading.)

3. Commit yourself to completing this book, always listening to the *still, small voice* within you that will set the perfect pace for your progress through the chapters.

4. Have fun! Remember, since you are the Wisdom of God, you already know all there is to know. These are simply tools to tickle your memory!

5. Allow yourself to transform your consciousness and to live an Abundant Life by practicing (Receiving and Giving) these GIFTS on an ongoing basis. Yes, it truly is all in the *allowing*. . . allowing ourselves to be guided by the Divine Essence within us. . . allowing ourselves to fall into and to be transformed by the loving embrace of the Goodness of Life!

The 5 GIFTS Chapters

The itinerary for this stage of your journey has been set and the 5 GIFTS are waiting for you. As you prepare to open them one by one, remember to take your time. Savor every discovery you make about yourself and your relationship to each GIFT, no matter how "small" any discovery may seem. Chapters 2 through 8 are designed to ignite your deepest realization of each of the 5 GIFTS, as well as opportunities to integrate each one into your daily being and doing, from the time your alarm clock goes off in the morning until you drift off to sleep at night. We can "know" a GIFT all we want, but without *giving it* we cannot activate its inherent transforming power to manifest the Abundance of God as our life!

Each of the 5 GIFTS chapters will contain five sections:

- An in-depth description of the GIFT
- A Mystic Speaks on the GIFT
- Personal Success Story: A Real Life Moment
- Give Your Gift Practice: Heart Opening Instructions
- Acknowledge Yourself: Give a Gift to You!

It's Time to Set Off

We're ready to begin our journey and we are starting on the perfect day . . . your birthday! Why? Because your birthday is a holy day that is unique to you. Your arrival on this planet is cause for an annual recognition of the day you were born. It is that special time to honor your courage and commitment to being here as the precious expression of God that you are. It is the day for acknowledging how important your life is to the grand tapestry of Life. As the beginning of your new year it is the perfect day to review the year gone by and to claim your heart's desires. And it is the ideal day for you to receive a message of a lifetime. The candles on your cake are waiting! . . .

CHAPTER 1

HAPPY BIRTHDAY!

Happy Birthday! The candles on your cake are glowing brightly. You are surrounded by family and friends and you have spent the entire day basking in the limelight. You've even pampered yourself with special little gifts on your day—sleeping in just a bit later, taking five more minutes with your pet, allowing yourself to skip your usual workout schedule, and indulging in a relaxed birthday celebration at the office.

As you get set to blow out the candles, an intention comes from deep within your soul. On the wind of your breath, you make this promise, "This year I am going to live an Abundant Life! I am dedicated to experiencing more health, more wholesome relationships, more money, and more opportunities to give the talents I have to give." The candle flames are extinguished and your resolve is firm.

After savoring the delicious cake and ice cream, you are invited to open your presents. The party of celebrants moves to the pile of gifts awaiting your attention. As you open one exciting gift after another you recognize that you are already experiencing abundance . . . and your year has only just begun!

You are so thoroughly enjoying this part of your birthday celebration that you didn't notice the Stranger enter the circle of friends around you. So intent are you on the pleasure of unwrapping each gift that you aren't aware of the hush that falls over your guests at the sight of this Being who has mysteriously appeared in their midst. You look up for a moment to convey gratitude to a friend for a beautiful piece of clothing and suddenly see what everyone else is seeing. There before you stands a luminous figure in a shimmering lavender floor-length cloak. The light from Its face

15

and hands is dazzling. You can't tell if It is male or female, human or divine. Before you have a chance to decide, this "person" puts five beautifully wrapped GIFTS in your lap.

Without speaking, the mysterious Stranger miraculously conveys to you this message: **"I have come to give you 5 GIFTS for your soul. These GIFTS are the answer to your birthday wish to live an Abundant Life. Receive them with the Love in which they are given. In and of themselves they are valuable ideas for your mind. They are also spiritual principles that will set your life on fire when they are fully understood and accepted in your heart. Their greatest value lies in their power to change your consciousness . . . and therefore your life! Know that it is only as you give these 5 GIFTS to yourself and others through continued practice that you will realize your soul's desire to live an Abundant Life. As you become a Divine Circulator of these GIFTS—receiving them and giving them—so you become the Divine Circulator of the Abundance of God."**

And with that, as suddenly as It had joined the party, the illumined figure disappears.

CHAPTER 2

GRATITUDE

Give Out

s you gaze at the 5 GIFTS before you, you notice that one package seems to be almost vibrating, as if it were trying to catch your attention and shout, "Open me first!" You remove it from among the others and, with quivering fingers holding onto the bright silver paper, you tug on the shimmering ribbon. The mysterious Visitor's earlier admonition that you can receive these GIFTS only if you are willing to continually give them reverberates in your ear. Lifting the lid of the box, you scan the ornate card that you discover inside:

> # GRATITUDE
>
> Through giving this GIFT
> you name your entire life a blessing!

GRATITUDE is the GIFT of being thankful. What a wondrous present to receive and to give! In living an Abundant Life, giving this GIFT becomes the prayer of the heart that opens your life to the riches contained in it. GRATITUDE is the door to the abundance of God and all of creation. Through its magical use, you begin to appreciate every wonder of your journey.

GRATITUDE is a love vibration. When we are grateful we exude a feeling tone of acceptance and appreciation. Thanksgiving allows us to connect to what we are experiencing from the heart space. It is when we move from our heads to our hearts that we open up to the sacred in all things and allow ourselves to feel a sense of oneness with all of life. And so in giving the GIFT of GRATITUDE, we become aware of the presence of God in all.

GRATITUDE is a distiller of emotions. When you give thanks you are purifying your emotional response to life by focusing on love and leaving fear, doubt, worry, shame and blame behind. The simple truth is that you cannot, at one and the same time, experience appreciation and any other emotional responses. As you continue to be grateful, the reactions that are lesser, darker or narrower tend to weaken and lose their momentum, leaving you free to be light and loving. In this state, awareness of the abundance of life is so easy to see and experience.

GRATITUDE is the great multiplier. Giving thanks and appreciating all that we have opens the door for us to have more. Jesus, the Christ, demonstrated this truth over and over in his ministry. It was after giving thanks that he was able to feed the 5,000 from a few loaves and fishes and still have much to spare. If you want more of something in your life, be grateful for what you have. The new age/ancient wisdom axiom is true: What you put your attention on grows. When you attend to something in GRATITUDE, that metaphysical law is activated, and you will experience more of it.

GRATITUDE puts you in the witness state. By giving thanks you disengage your panel of internal judges—that committee that is so ready to condemn or label the person or circumstance as anything but "good." Freed from judging and aligned with the gift of the experience, you will find yourself lifted into a new and welcome perspective as beholder of the greater divine perfection and pattern of your life. You come into harmony with your essence and God's vision for your life when you can detach from the conditions of your life by appreciating all of them—the good and the *apparently* not-so-good. Even circumstances that appear to be out of sync with your expectations (the relationship failed, another person got the job, the flu didn't stop when you were ready to be well) will lose their labels of "bad," "ain't it awful!" or "what did I do wrong?" under the clarifying rays of a grateful heart. Your heart is now open and receptive to the gifts of God to which you would have been blind in your former, limited state of consciousness.

GRATITUDE is the grace that re-visions our linear lives, working magic with every strand of past, present and future. When we are grateful for the persons and events from our past, we know we have completed the forgiveness process. (We will take an in-depth look at this process in later chapters.) *Being grateful for what was* allows us to have all of our selves available in the present moment. Only when we are unencumbered by blame, shame, resentment or guilt—negative attachments to our past— can we make sense out of the past, see its patterns, feel its rhythms, and readily extract the pearls of wisdom and grace from our past experiences. We are now indeed free to be all that we are created to be.

Being thankful for what is at this present moment keeps us in acceptance of what we are actually experiencing right now, without judgment. In that detached state we can truly know that the Holy is present in all things, now. By giving thanks we name each circumstance, each person, a blessing in our lives. *Being thankful for what will be* before we actually experience it grants us the consciousness to receive that which we desire. An attitude of GRATITUDE is a key element in moving us to a state of receptivity. In that place of being receptive to our good, we move from perceived limitations into the passion of possibilities, without attachment to "how" our good is to be manifested. In GRATITUDE, we can let go and let God bring about our desired outcome.

By giving and receiving GRATITUDE, we acknowledge the truth: *All life is a **Gift**.* Thank you, God!

A Mystic Speaks on Gratitude

Christian D. Larson
from *The Pathway of Roses*

When we feel that God will give us anything we may ask for,
that there is no doubt about it whatever, we cannot otherwise but give
expression to the very soul of gratitude, and this gratitude is both
limitless and endless;
it is the soul's eternal thanksgiving.
To live in the spirit of that prayer that is ever asking God for everything,
that believes that God is giving everything,
and that is constantly giving thanks to God for everything, is, in itself,
a life of highest joy. In such a life, everything is being taken
to a higher ground,
because we are manifesting in body, mind and soul,
more and more of the likeness of God. Personal existence is becoming
ideal existence, while the soul is living in the full conscious realization
of God's own beautiful world.

Two Personal Success Stories

A Real Life Moment Of
GRATITUDE

Seeing Through a Grateful Heart
by Tina Fox

The past year had been particularly difficult for Michael, my partner, and me. We had reached a point in our relationship where we were reevaluating whether we should continue being together. Neither one of us could point to any one thing in particular. Maybe it was an accumulation of "the little things" over the past 18 years we'd spent together, or maybe it was just the gradual growing apart that some people do. What we did know, and painfully so, was that over the past few months our relationship had deteriorated to the point of almost constant sniping, sarcasm, anger or simple blank apathy.

After one particularly bitter encounter, I sat on the stairs in our living room and told Michael that I was unwilling to do this anymore and that I thought it was time to put an end to the pain. If that meant breaking up and going our separate ways, so be it. We both retreated to our respective parts of the house to think it over.

It was the beginning of the Christmas season and Michael's company was having their annual Christmas party the next evening. The next day, Michael called me from work and, in his way of making a peace offering, asked me if I would be willing to come to the party with him. I agreed, but in retrospect it's clear that we were not ready to release the anger and bitterness that had been building up between us.

That night, although we were trying to be civil, we took several verbal jabs at each other while getting ready for the party. By the time both of us were ready to leave we were primed for battle. It was raining, we were late, and we had to drive more than 20 miles through stop-and-go traffic to get to the party venue. About ten miles from our destination, the "low gasoline" warning buzzer sounded. "Great," I thought, "now we're about to run out of gas!" I watched as Michael passed up gas station after gas station because it either wasn't the right brand or the gas station was on the wrong side of the street. I sat there, furious, saying nothing, gathering energy for the next verbal attack. And then, suddenly, it hit me. What *was* I so upset about? I was afraid . . . but of what? The car running out of gas? I was angry . . . but about what? That Michael did things differently than I did? Who was I to think that ego-me had all of the answers? I took a deep breath and I looked around me. Everything slowed down.

It was raining and the raindrops made a beautiful pattern as they hit the windshield and exploded on impact. The streetlights and the car taillights glowed and reflected off the wet pavement—red streaks, white streaks. I turned and looked at Michael, and I was filled with such gratitude—for that moment, for all of the moments we had spent together, for his uniqueness, for all of his qualities. And, from a very different emotional place than I had been in just a few moments before, I said, "You know, Michael, we do things totally differently. And it's O.K."

I could feel the smile creeping across my face and I was filled with love. Instead of reacting with sarcasm, he looked over at me and it felt as if an enormous bubble of tension and anger had burst. We were looking at each other, really looking at each other, and seeing one another for the first time in a long time.

Underneath all of the hurt, the disappointment, the anger, the resentment, the need to be right, there was still love. And I knew in that moment that as long as we could find our way to the love we really felt, we could find our way back to one another.

I would be lying if I said that everything was perfect after that. But that sudden realization of gratitude did give us a starting point that only moments before had felt out of the question. That night marked the beginning of our building a bridge of reconciliation. And, to me, the energy of feeling grateful for who and what Michael really was, instead of feeling disappointed that he didn't fit the illusion of who and what I wanted him to be, was the beginning of building that bridge.

My Journey into Gratitude
by Kamin Bell

Gratitude is a continual process, one in which I must constantly rise above "the seen" and focus on "the unseen" and on the many blessings in my life.

As a manager of a small team within a medium-sized company, I was faced with significant inequities in pay. Earlier this year, a manager's position in my department became vacant. It was this manager's job to oversee a team with a different set of skills than my own. I participated in the selection process to fill this position. One day the recruiter let slip the salary that was going to be offered to the individual who got the job. It was close to $10,000 more than I was making, and I had been with the company nearly three years. Although I was stunned by that figure, I was not completely surprised because I had had an inkling that the members of the other team were paid more than my team members.

The following day I mentioned this inequity to my boss. He commented that the difference wasn't really that great and that the market dictated what the new manager would be paid. I was upset because I felt that my background and experience were more extensive than the new manager's, but I kept silent, brooding all the while.

Thankfully, the *5 GIFTS for an Abundant Life!*™ course started soon after this had occurred because I was brought face to face with Gratitude—the challenge of learning to be grateful for everything in my life, even my struggles. After a couple of weeks of meditations led by Reverend Diane, readings on gratitude and thankfulness, and keeping a gratitude journal, I was actually able to feel grateful for this situation. Of course, it didn't happen overnight. My resentments and hurt over not being recognized at the same level as the "new guy" were deep. But I became centered in class on God being my source and being grateful for all that I had been given. I began to refocus my energies on my team and consciously improve my leadership skills. I became truly thankful for this and all of the other opportunities in my life.

My gratefulness was tested several months later when a co-worker from another department mentioned that my newly-hired peer had been promoted to a level higher than mine. Furthermore, his promotion had been given in secret a month earlier, without any announcement to the department. I hid my surprise and dismay from my co-worker but quickly began to seethe with anger. I asked another manager within our department if he knew about the promotion and he didn't. Together we confronted our boss and he did not initially admit to the promotion. He did on the following day, however, with the excuse that it had been a necessary job recalibration: the manager's title had been "adjusted" based on his experience.

At that moment, the only thing in my awareness was the fact

that this new manager's experience was less than mine. Gratitude for my boss was nowhere to be found, not then and not for the several weeks that followed. However, I still remained grateful for my team and for my position as their manager. I kept putting all of my energies into them and it showed—they became one of the most productive teams in the company. But my heart still hurt because I hadn't been promoted; I was still angry at my boss, and I disliked the other manager.

Weeks later, at a church service, the minister asked for those who had unforgivingness in their hearts toward someone to raise their hands. I did. As he prayed over us, I did an exercise I had learned in the *5 GIFTS* course and let the light in my heart dissolve the darkness, hurt and anger. I let it go. What emerged was love and thankfulness. I could clearly see that my attitude toward my boss had suffered during this time and that, although I was still managing my team well, I hadn't been a great employee. I was able to feel truly thankful I still had a job as well as the opportunity to rectify my part in my relationship with my boss.

When I returned to work that week my attitude was one of gratefulness and service. I remembered that I had prayed for the managerial position I was in and that God had given it to me. I had lost sight of who was really in charge of my life and my career. Within a few days I had a meeting with my boss and apologized for my attitude and for having been focused on the wrong things. We spoke several times over the next few days and I was respectfully very open and honest, not leaving room for even a single "I wish I'd said . . ."

As I began to focus on being thankful not just for my team but also for my boss and the other manager, peace and joy filled my thoughts. I wasn't dreading work or being around them. Love filled my heart and I became a better manager and co-worker. With my focus on serving my boss and the company better, I began to recognize my worth as an employee and the fact that I had even more to offer the company. I started to look for openings in other departments. When I found one I advised my boss, according to company policy, that I would be applying for it. He reluctantly agreed. It turned out that I didn't get that position, but once again I advised him that I would be applying for a different position that had become available. He seemed genuinely disappointed and hurt and asked what it would take to keep me as a team manager in his department. After great consideration, I wrote down exactly what title and salary I wanted. My request is currently under review.

The extraordinary thing about what has transpired is that it all comes back to the practice of gratitude. I had gotten caught up in wanting what someone else had and not being grateful for what I had been entrusted with. Gratitude must be visited regularly, daily, and if necessary, minute by minute. I frequently go back to the tools I learned in class to be grateful for the whole of my life, not just those things I can control. Regardless of what others may or may not do, or what the future holds, I remind myself constantly that God is my source and that I am truly blessed. No matter what the outcome concerning the job, I've received the most important promotion of all—a promotion to a more open heart and a deeper consciousness of love in my entire life. I am so grateful for my life and all that is in it! [P.S. Kamin got her promotion and is very grateful!]

Give Your Gift PRACTICE

Heart Opening Instructions
for
GRATITUDE

The GIFT of GRATITUDE comes with a set of directions. They are intended to help you take steps in your daily "doings" toward achieving an Abundant Life. Now is your time to commit to these simple suggestions, to call your Prosperity Prayer Partner and agree to support each other in these practices, and to be fully available for shifts in your consciousness.

WARNING: Activating this spiritual practice of thankfulness—or any of the other four GIFTS—may lead to instant bliss and abundance. Or, you may find yourself experiencing what appears to be a breakdown of your life. Please note that both of these responses to your intention to change your consciousness to one of being abundant can *and need* to be expected. When we actively desire to grow spiritually into our possibilities, we challenge the belief systems that have held our old way of being in place. We shake the very core of our foundation—and the entrenched pylons are resistant to change. If that sense of resistance or breakdown occurs, welcome it, love it and name it a sure sign that you are on the right path to transformation. Do not use it as a "sign" or excuse to abandon the work and resign yourself to being stuck. That appearance of what seems like a negative reaction to your vision of change is actually an invitation and an opportunity to strengthen your resolve and build your spiritual muscle. Give thanks and be grateful for this sign that you are indeed changing into a greater you! Also . . . even though we may not understand it at the time, we are always moving toward our Greater Good. It may take some time for this to become apparent, but it is always the case.

Gratitude Journal

For the next five weeks make the commitment to write down five gifts you are grateful for each day. Practice this simple yet enormously effective way to consciously acknowledge the giving-ness of God in your life. A blessing of keeping a gratitude journal is that during those times when life is feeling tough you have concrete evidence to remind yourself of all the gifts you have been given.

Be sure to include the most ordinary as well as the extraordinary gifts of daily living. Here are some examples:

1. Thank you for the sunshine this morning.
2. I am so grateful for my son's giggle.
3. I am so glad for the love and support of my Prosperity Prayer Partner.
4. I am grateful that the repairman came between the hours he promised.
5. Thank you for the stamps I found in the drawer so that I could mail out that letter on time.

Create a *ritual time* to do this quick and easy practice of GRATITUDE, perhaps in the evening right before bed. Keep it simple, keep your commitment and keep your resolve to live an Abundant Life through giving the GIFT of GRATITUDE.

Grace Before Meals

Creating a ritualized time to say "Thanks" during each day is to "pray without ceasing," to express appreciation and open your heart to the good of God. One simple way to do this is to attach the practice of GRATITUDE to an activity we do daily—eating. Make the commitment to give thanks before each meal. Blessing your food puts you in contact with the Source of it, those who grew it, prepared it, served it, as well as your own body and the nourishment you are giving it. Giving thanks for your meal also allows you to be in conscious connection with those with whom you are sharing your meal. You are blessing a blessing and naming it all a GIFT for an Abundant Life.

Use any of the simple blessings below or, better yet, create your own. Make it short, sweet and different each time. Say it out loud or silently. Take a moment to quiet yourself and then just let yourself speak whatever you are grateful for in the moment. When you are with others, consider holding hands around the table and initiating a group blessing of your meal. Going around the table, each person makes a brief contribution to the meal blessing or says "Pass." When it gets back to you, offer a closing thought and a "Thank You." You may be quite pleasantly surprised by the effect of this simple group activity.

Let's give thanks to the Source for this nourishment. Knowing that life renews itself, we eat this food with gladness and gratitude. Amen.

Joyfully, we give thanks for this food, and for the many blessings that so richly enhance our lives this day. Namasté.

With gratitude of heart and mind, we bless this meal, knowing that it gives life to life. And so it is.

Go Ahead ... Make Someone's Day

Give yourself a beautiful gift by giving away your appreciation. Tell the first person you see every day one reason why you're grateful for her or him. And when you feel the joy you've unleashed, you will open yourself up to give and receive so much more!

ACKNOWLEDGE YOURSELF

Giving the GIFT of GRATITUDE
to You!

Name one gift you can give yourself in acknowledgment for being the fabulous, abundant, grateful Being that you are. . . . And do it! Begin with identifying an activity you have been wanting to do but putting off. Is it taking a walk on the beach or through the park without the kids? Shooting hoops with the guys, going to lunch with a friend, or sitting down with a good novel? Or is it having a date night with your love? Whatever it may be, simply know this: Giving to yourself is the greatest GIFT you can give!

CHAPTER 3

Setting
INTENTIONS
Give In

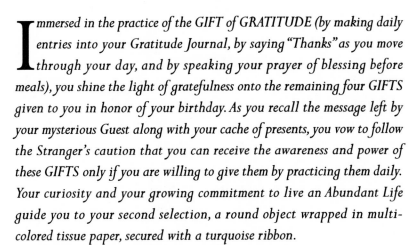

*I*mmersed in the practice of the GIFT of GRATITUDE (by making daily entries into your Gratitude Journal, by saying "Thanks" as you move through your day, and by speaking your prayer of blessing before meals), you shine the light of gratefulness onto the remaining four GIFTS given to you in honor of your birthday. As you recall the message left by your mysterious Guest along with your cache of presents, you vow to follow the Stranger's caution that you can receive the awareness and power of these GIFTS only if you are willing to give them by practicing them daily. Your curiosity and your growing commitment to live an Abundant Life guide you to your second selection, a round object wrapped in multi-colored tissue paper, secured with a turquoise ribbon.

Unwrapping the GIFT from its soft crinkling paper, you discover a circular hoop lashed all around in leather, with magnificent bird feathers and earth-toned beads hanging like a tail down one side. In the very center of the circle is an aqua gemstone that is connected to the rim by an intricate pattern of woven string reminding you of a spider's web. You recognize this GIFT symbol as a Native American Dream Catcher. The two sides of the tag that accompanies the GIFT read . . .

<table>
<tr><td>

Instructions for

The GIFT
of
INTENTIONS

</td><td>

Dream...
Do...
Detach...

Through giving
this GIFT
you create your
Life Experience!

</td></tr>
</table>

One of the greatest privileges we have as human beings is the ability to choose. Conscious choice is a uniquely human quality. We are the sole creatures on this planet that can design our lives entirely by *choosing* what we will focus our attention upon. It is our honor, as well as our duty, to exercise this power of choice by setting and manifesting our INTENTIONS.

There is a metaphysical law that is activated when we make a choice. It is the Law of Manifestation (also known as the Law of Cause and Effect). This law states that *as a man thinketh so shall it be*. What we choose to think creates our experience. Through our thinking (cause) we create our reality (effect). From the realm of the invisible we bring our thoughts—our intentions—into form. We make them visible.

The Law of Manifestation continuously responds to our thoughts, both conscious and unconscious. By becoming aware and choosing what to think we are designing our lives! And by **not** choosing (which means we are letting our thoughts be whatever comes into our minds) we are *still* designing our lives. Further, when we dwell on a condition that we do not want instead of what we do want, we are choosing that unwanted condition by default. When we realize that all of these approaches constitute a choice, we can begin to understand why it is that we have experiences (circumstances, people, emotional challenges) in our lives that we don't want. These experiences are created by unconscious thoughts that we no longer want but that are left over from some time in our past. These experiences still manifest in our lives because we have not set an *intention* for something new to take their place. So it is through using the powerful GIFT of INTENTIONS (clearly focused choice) that we create whatever we want in our lives.

The irony is that most of us do not even know that we have this power, this GIFT. Or, if we do, we often shrink back in fear of using it because somewhere inside we don't think we're worthy of having what we desire.

Let's give ourselves a moment here to digest this information. I invite you to start by taking a long, slow, deep breath. And as you exhale, feel yourself releasing any tension that came up when you read the last two paragraphs. Now, let's gently drop together beneath the surface of the everyday concepts we hold. One such concept is that, when you or I have an idea, that idea originates with us. It is your idea or my idea, your choice or my choice. The truth is "our ideas" do not originate with us—they are the very thoughts of God. These God Thoughts are simply available to all of us and they are ready at any time to move through us and to take form. As humans we serve as the vehicles through which thoughts may express. Our INTENTIONS, then, are always Divine Ideas, and it is by our willingness to have them manifest through us that we become co-creators with Spirit.

Picture it this way: We are swimming in the Mind of God. And in that Mind are all of the ideas and thoughts that have ever been or ever will be manifested into form. In order for **any** of God's ideas to come into form, it needs one of our minds to express it . . . for *we are the vehicles through which God reveals Itself*. For example, Einstein was the mind that said "Yes" to the Divine Idea of Relativity. Mozart said "Yes" to the Divine Thought of "Eine Kleine Nachtmusik," and Martin Luther King said "Yes" to the Holy Concept of "I Have a Dream."

Imagine that, as you are swimming in the Mind of God, the Divine Ideas are constantly being communicated to you as INTENTIONS through the holy languages of imagination and inspiration. Realize that one of the compelling aspects of Spirit is Its movement from the invisible to the visible, bringing Its pure possibility into form. Realize also that imagination and inspiration are the languages of your Mind of the Heart, not the mind of your mind.

Remember the times when you've had a great idea? When, out of the blue, some wonderful inspiration came to you? When your imagination got triggered and you became intent upon doing something? The place in you where that process happens is the place of non-linear, non-judgmental, illogical, free-form *"Aha!"* It is the space where possibilities have a chance to bloom without the intrusion of logic, limiting beliefs or past experiences. We've each had many such Spirit knocks-on-the-door to the Mind of our Heart. Which leads us to the first instruction accompanying this GIFT. . .

Dream . . .

A dream came to me one day when my husband and I were traveling in Hawaii several years ago. We spent six weeks touring the Islands and soaking up the sun on every beach we could find. And the only thing that was missing on that dream trip of a lifetime was the comfort of a good beach chair—the grass mats provided by our hotels just didn't cut it! During one morning meditation the idea came to me to create a collapsible beach chair that was lightweight and easy to carry. My idea was to invent a portable chair patterned after the tents campers use, featuring segments of featherweight poles that would click together to hold the sturdy fabric of the chair seat and back. When collapsed, all the components would fit into a tidy lightweight tote with a cushioned strap you could sling over your shoulder for easy transport.

As I came out of meditation, inspiration ignited my imagination, and suddenly I saw the whole thing . . . the manufactured chair in a selection of colors, the packaging design, the plan for the marketing campaign, and millions of people using my invention. Within an hour, I had "dreamed" myself all the way into a very wealthy, successful inventor who was contributing to the well-being of millions of beach goers. I had caught God's Idea in the Mind of my Heart and was setting my INTENTION to manifest it. To realize an Abundant Life, dreaming is the essential first aspect of INTENTION Setting. The popular Dream Catcher of Native American origin reminds us to practice the art of collecting the dreams (Divine Ideas) of God. Hung above your bed, its purpose is to serve as the web that catches your bad dreams and releases them, while securely holding your good dreams for you to remember and review. And what does it mean *to dream*?

- *To dream* is to open your self to the thoughts of God.
- *To dream* is to become consciously aware of the desires of God that want to come through you.
- *To dream* is to choose one thought and say "Yes" to it.
- *To dream* is to surrender into the Mind of your Heart, where the invisible Divine Idea can find fertile soil to grow and become, no matter what the external circumstances.
- *To dream* is to step beyond what is . . . to what can be.
- *To dream* is to dance in the realm of all possibilities, to step outside the box, to try on, to stretch and grow, to choose to be a vehicle of Holy Manifestation.
- *To dream* is the first step of receiving the GIFT of INTENTIONS.

Do . . .

This second action word on the gift card is one with which we feel most familiar. In our busy lives we are constantly doing, doing, doing. Our "doing" is outer directed. It is focused on the world of effects and circumstances where we have been taught to believe that we can "make it happen" through willpower and our physical and mental focus. However, more often than not, what we tend to experience is a temporary "fix" or a need to focus and work so hard to sustain the goal that it takes all our waking energy to achieve it.

The *Do* instruction for the GIFT of Setting INTENTIONS is altogether different from that scenario. This *doing* is inner directed. This *do* asks us to give our assent to what is wanting to flow through us . . . to say "Yes" to that Divine Idea. It mandates focusing our attention on building a safe, nurturing, internal place for the Seedling INTENTION to take root and sprout. This *doing* may seem inactive, even passive. But in fact it is a potent action requiring the ideal, nurturing environment of our internal focus and attention. From this perspective, **Do . . .** means

- *Do* allow INTENTIONS to grow out of your Dreams.
- *Do* cultivate an undying trust in your intuition and let its voice of inspiration guide you.
- *Do* resist any temptation to limit your INTENTIONS by trying to figure out "how" they will manifest. (The choosing is up to you; the "how" is up to God.)
- *Do* stay out of the mind of your mind where arguments against your INTENTIONS—and against you as the perfect instrument for their manifestation—are brewing.
- *Do* put your attention on the present and what you are guided to do *now*.
- *Do* keep your attention on the essence of the INTENTION, not the details.
- *Do* pray affirmatively, knowing that contained within this INTENTION is everything necessary for its complete revelation into form.
- *Do* keep your newly born creation to yourself. Hold it quietly in the radiance of your heart, just as you would a baby, until it is strong enough to stand on its own.

I was brimming over with excitement about my beach chair

idea. I felt I just had to tell my husband how I planned to deliver glorious and portable back support to traveling beach goers and make millions. Fresh from setting my INTENTION, I cornered my mate at the kitchen table where he was buried behind the morning paper. "Honey," I began, "guess what? I have this great idea. . . ." My enthusiasm was running high, but it fell flat as he met my newly-birthed idea with staunch skepticism and negativity. How on earth did I plan to carry this idea out? Where was I going to find a design engineer, a manufacturing company, a package design firm? And how did I think I was going to find the money to finance this little fancy? "You are a therapist and counselor, not a product designer," he continued. "Aren't you stepping way out of your field?" I was devastated . . . yet part of me was convinced that he was speaking the truth. Who was I, anyway, to have such a crazy idea? How would I get these things manufactured and to market? Who did I think I was? And so, after feebly running my idea by another family member and then a close friend only to receive the same kinds of challenging questions and disbelief, I slowly let the whole idea go.

Do . . . allow your dreams to be nourished in the space of silence and wonderment for as long as they need. *Do* . . . respect the magic of manifestation, as God's Thoughts become your co-ideas, your co-plans, then your co-creations, all in their own true time. Which leads us to the last word of the instructions for this GIFT.

Detach ...
The difference between goals and INTENTIONS for our purposes is that goals are those declarations to which we have added attachments. In traditional goal setting we choose what we are going to accomplish and then we list specific objectives that tell

us how, when and by what means we will achieve these goals. INTENTIONS, on the other hand, have no added attachments beyond our agreement to serve as the vehicle through which they will manifest. When we set our INTENTION our job is to *allow* that process to move through us without attachment to the outcome.

. . . It was about 18 months later that I was leafing through an in-flight catalog and saw, featured in full color, the beach chair I had dreamed and intended for a short while. The Divine Idea had found a willing mind and soul through which to bring about this beach-y dream. I had given up in the belief that I was too small (and dumb and inexperienced and broke) to have it come through me. I had negatively "detached" myself from the beach chair idea by letting my ego shut down in fear and doubt. But this negative detachment is far from the soulful leap of faith we're talking about. Here *Detach* means to let go of any concern about how an idea will come about.

Rather than *Do* what my Mind of the Heart was asking (hold the space for the idea to take form), I had allowed my beach chair dream to be trampled by who, how, when and where concerns before it had a chance to take root, thereby denying God Its part in our co-creation. This final step of the INTENTION Setting process is captured in a phrase we're all familiar with: "Let go and let God." By surrendering the "how" to God, we are free to faithfully keep our attention on the essence of our INTENTIONS. As we practice *letting God*, our trust inevitably grows. And so does our ease and dedication in listening to our intuitive voice. Spoken through inspiration, that voice is there guiding us moment by moment to the realization of God's Idea. It is then in true partnership that we can give the GIFT of INTENTIONS.

A Mystic Speaks on Setting Intentions

Ernest Holmes

from *The Science of Mind*

One of the most important things for us to remember is that we are always causing something to be created for us. And that whatever cause we have set in motion must produce some kind of effect. Are we producing the effects we should like to experience? The creative process will go on willy nilly. We cannot beat Nature at her own games for we are some part of the game She is playing. Shall the result, in our lives, be a comedy or a tragedy? We are given the Will to decide the issue.

We should carefully consider whether we are willing to experience the results of our thoughts. There should never be any hurt in them, for ourselves or for anyone else. We may be sure that if there is hurt for others there must also be hurt for ourselves. As we sow, so we must reap, but here is no real limitation, for the Creative Life wishes us to have all that we can use. If we keep our thought fixed upon the idea that this Energy, which is also Intelligence, is now taking the form of some desire in our lives, then it will begin to take this form. If we change the desire then It will change the form. Therefore, there must be a definite purpose in our imagination.

We are so One with the Whole that what is true of It is also true of us. We are one with unmanifest Substance whose business it is to forever take form and we are one with the Law which gives form. The entire order is one of spontaneous being and spontaneous manifestation. The Law follows the word just as the word follows the desire. The desire arises from the necessity of the Universe to become self-expressed. . . .

Personal Success Story

A Real Life Moment Of
Setting INTENTION

The e-Power of Intention Setting
by Mo Rafael

One chilly morning in late November I was getting dressed for the day. As I started to put on my boots I thought I heard, "Are you *sure* you want to wear your boots today?" Certain that I hadn't really heard any such thing, I proceeded to pull on my left boot. And when I was about to pick up my right one the question came again. This time I knew I'd heard what I thought I'd heard, but I was so nonplussed that I just kept on doing what I was doing. Finally, with boots now on both feet I unmistakably heard the question for the third time, "Are you *sure* you want to wear your boots today?" I don't know if I spoke my answer out loud or just thought it in my head, but I clearly remember my response, "Yes I do. I'm cold, and my boots keep my feet warm!"

A few hours later, still wearing my boots, I lost my footing and took a whopping spill on my garage floor. The sound of the impact wasn't pretty . . . I'd broken my left kneecap. During the six weeks of near immobility following open knee surgery and the many weeks of painful rehab, I had plenty of time to think back to that morning . . . to feel sorry for myself, to rue and regret my stonewalling, and to be angry with myself for not heeding the voice of my intuition. Oh so fortunately, I was taking a Prosperity class with Reverend Diane during that same time period. One

44

of the fundamental principles that class covered was the power of intention: clearly setting one's intention as opposed to letting old habits have their same old way with us. So I knew that if I didn't want to get stuck in that familiar old negative emotional cycle of self-pity, remorse and anger turned inward, I could consciously make the choice to move in a positive direction instead. And, with the prayer and focus of the class as support, that is what I did. I set these intentions: to accept what had happened, to open to the blessings of being slowed down, to learn to ask for help when I needed it (a tough one for me!), and to pay attention to my inner voice—no matter how trivial its promptings might seem.

At first I wondered how I was going to manage to keep that commitment to myself because I was so accustomed to not being tuned into or paying attention to my intuition, or to arguing with it and overruling it. But the blessing of my broken kneecap was that it was "in my face" all the time. Every step I took and every activity I could no longer do with ease—or even without pain—reminded me that I'd set my intention to pay attention to my intuition. I can honestly and joyfully say that the strength of setting my intention (bolstered by the constant motivation of a dysfunctional body part I'd so much taken for granted) was what got me "over to the other side," i.e., to doing exactly what I'd set my intention on. I spent almost no time on a learning curve of "trying to learn how to do it." Instead, I found myself simply honoring my intention without question . . . and frequently being amazed by how easily I could do that. I was equally amazed by the harvest of small miracles that I reaped from following my intuition: catching someone on the phone who was just on her way out of town for three weeks; taking a book off my bookshelf and finding a receipt I'd been looking for for nearly a month; stopping by a secondhand store I'd never been to before and finding a chair to match one a friend had left me when she'd moved. . .

But imagine my surprise when a "large miracle" came to pass about five months after my accident. I sauntered in the door after church one Sunday in April and couldn't wait to sit down to a big, leisurely breakfast. Before I even got my hand on the refrigerator door I heard my intuitive voice say "Go to Earth Day." Immediately, I had a myriad of excuses and rationalizations for not following through on my intention to follow my intuition: "I really don't like crowds!" "Been there, done that . . ." and "Parking will be impossible!" topped the list. But the flow of energy from having firmly set and consistently followed my intention thus far just overpowered them all. . . . Next thing I knew I was saying goodbye to my roommate and heading out the door with a protein bar in hand.

Hmmm . . . the traffic wasn't too bad, the parking was "impossible" except for the spot quite close to the entrance to Balboa Park that I happened to score, and the crowds were thick but, when I walked at my chosen pace, a path seemed to open just ahead of me. O.K., there I was. "But what for?" I wondered! I looked around and my gaze fell on a stack of green flyers weighted down against the light breeze with a beach rock: Win a Free Car Today! Fully Electric—Zero Emissions. "Really? . . ."

So I worked my way down to the lower end of the park. And there it was . . . a small Ford named the *"Think" Neighbor*. It was a cute little blue car, but it was truly the funniest-looking thing I'd seen poised on a platform since Bullwinkle. (During my childhood a statue of Bullwinkle—of Bullwinkle and Rocky fame—had made fun of the Las Vegas showgirl figure that revolved on a platform above Sunset Boulevard right across the street.) In fact, the oddity of the Ford Think "on high" reminded me so fondly of the Bullwinkle that I set my intention then and there to win the car.

There were a lot of people standing around looking at the car, and another crowd of people hovering around the booth where you entered the drawing. After waiting in line to pick up an entry form, I was shocked to discover that you first had to answer the ten questions on the entry sheet and get all answers correct in order to even enter the drawing.

In dismay, I decided to call it quits. This was too much! But no sooner had I taken several determined steps toward the park exit than my intention pulled me right back. It took me another 30 minutes to make the rounds from booth to booth to get the answers to those darn questions. But finally I walked my answer sheet back to the drawing booth, had my answers checked, and was given the go-ahead, at last, to enter the drawing. Intention followed through on, I headed home.

I learned the news the next morning. . . . YES, I was the proud new owner of an adorable, brand new, four-passenger electric car.

P.S. This funny-looking car, by the way, gives a whole new meaning to the term "joy-riding." Heads turn and a smile lights up every face I pass when I go putt-putting down the streets of my hometown (Encinitas, California) at the top speed of 25 miles per hour in the "e-buggy!"

Give Your Gift PRACTICE

Heart Opening Instructions
for
Setting INTENTIONS

MIND OF THE HEART MAP:
My Divine Intentions

Call your Prosperity Prayer Partner and make a date to do this exercise together. Prepare by reviewing the following instructions and gathering the materials you'll need. Most importantly, you will want to prepare your consciousness by practicing moving your attention from the mind of your mind to the Mind of your Heart. A simple way to do this is to get quiet and place your attention on your physical brain. Then consciously move your attention down to the area of your physical heart. As you practice, notice how you can actually feel the difference in your body when you move your attention out of your head and into your heart space. When your attention is in the Mind of your Heart you are connecting to the realm of All Possibilities and can fully access the dream opportunities waiting for you there.

Supplies you'll need:

- Large poster board or another medium of your choice (One person in a 5 GIFTS class used a wire photo stand with eight arms and put her Divine Intentions on each extension.)

- Colored pens, pencils, paints or other media to color-code each Life Dimension
- An open Mind of the Heart

You may be familiar with Treasure Mapping or Mind Mapping. These are both exercises to assist you in tapping into your dreams and/or creative ideas. The following Heart Opener is a little different from each of them yet draws on the power of both. The key idea in creating a **Mind of the Heart Map** is to begin with Who you are in the center of your map . . . your *I AM*. (See Illustration on page 51.) The title *I AM* is God's name for you. No one else can claim it.

Draw a heart around your *I AM* in any color that reminds you that this exercise is to come from the Mind of your Heart. Next, surround the central *I AM* heart with eight more hearts, each in a different color. Label each one with a Life Dimension. The eight Life Dimensions are

- Spiritual Growth
- Career
- Family Relationships
- Finances/Investments
- Fun/Play
- Health/Well Being
- Love/Friendship
- Personal Growth/Education

Now comes the fun part that you do with your Prosperity Prayer Partner. Together, take ten minutes to go into meditation and connect with the Divine Intelligence within which you are immersed. Allow yourselves to bring your attention into the Mind of Your Heart as you surrender any preconceived ideas of past desires or any thoughts of limitation that may come up. Relax deeply and allow yourselves to listen to your inner Voice of Inspiration. When you complete the meditation, remain in the silence and let yourself be drawn to one of the Life Dimension hearts on your Map. Begin to create "rays" of INTENTIONS emerging from that heart, each one expressing a specific intention that you hold for yourself in that Life Dimension. Remaining in an open-hearted mode and deeply connected to the Divine Ideas that want to come through you, continue this exercise, creating eight rays of INTENTIONS around each Life Dimension. NOTE: Create each Life Dimension in a different color so that you can easily refer back to them later.

When you feel complete, be sure to date your **Mind of the Heart Map**. Take a few moments to feel delight in all that you've accomplished and to claim every one of your INTENTIONS as your Divine Co-creation. Then you can return to the meditative space and wait until your partner has also completed her/his **Mind of the Heart Map**. And when both of you have finished, I invite you to affirm in prayer that, without knowing "how," you know and trust that these INTENTIONS are fulfilled by That which inspired them in you.

MIND OF THE HEART MAP
My Divine Intentions
Date _____

DIVINE INTENTIONS
Above the "Ray" Line
   e.g. Hike once a quarter

QUALITIES OF GOD
Below the "Ray" Line
   e.g. Serenity, Beauty, Love,
   Harmony, Abundance, Peace

LIFE DIMENSIONS (Heart)
Spiritual Growth
Career
Family Relationships
Finances/Investments
Fun/Play
Health/Well Being
Love/Friendship
Personal Growth/Education

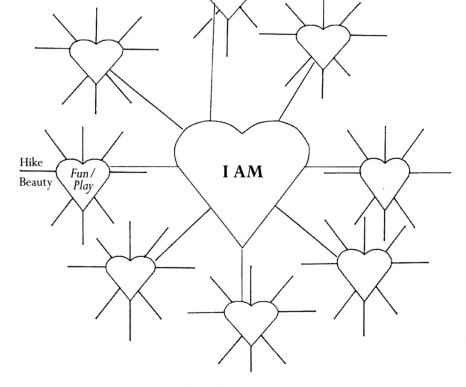

Hike
Beauty
Fun/Play

I AM

Create minimum of eight "Rays" out from every Life Dimension.
Color code each Life Dimension and its Divine Intention "Rays."
Create the "Rays" anchored in meditation in the Mind of your Heart.

ACKNOWLEDGE YOURSELF

Giving the GIFT of Setting INTENTIONS to You!

Celebrate your receiving and giving of the GIFT of Setting INTENTIONS with your Prosperity Prayer Partner. Identify one "ray" radiating out from the Fun/Play Life Dimension on your **Mind of the Heart Map**. If two can participate in the activity, set a date and time to manifest this Divine Idea. If it's an idea for one, ask for your Prosperity Prayer Partner's support in allowing it to come into manifestation through you in the next seven days. Enjoy the goodness of co-creation with God!

CHAPTER 4

Manifesting INTENTIONS

Give & Receive

Your "cup runneth over"—your banquet table is laden with an abundance of wonderful desires! From the realm of all possibilities, you have used your imagination and Divine Inspiration to claim the Holy Ideas that want to express through you in eight areas of your life. And you have allowed one of those INTENTIONS from the Life Dimension of *Fun/Play* on the **Mind of the Heart Map** to manifest into your life as a reward for surrendering to the Spirit's idea of who you are. Now what?

Let's find out how to use this map. You've certainly noticed that it looks nothing like the ones you keep in your glove compartment. Nowhere will you find a highway, byway or side street on the face of it. It doesn't lay out the routes you need to take to attain your dreams. It doesn't show you where to turn or how far to go down any given road. Your map is a topographic map of your desires (dreams) delineating the contours and features (dimensions) of your life. By its very nature it is an aerial or I AM view of your life. In order to harness the power of this map you must activate the final instruction for the GIFT of INTENTIONS: *Detach.* By staying on the mountaintop of your I AM, you let God do the work of manifesting your intended outcomes.

In *The Seven Spiritual Laws of Success,* Deepak Chopra writes "One characteristic of the field of all possibilities is infinite correlation. The field can orchestrate an infinity of space-time events to bring about the outcome that is intended. But when you are attached, your intention gets locked into a rigid mindset and you lose the fluidity, the creativity, and the spontaneity inherent in the field. When you get attached, you freeze your desire from that infinite fluidity and flexibility into a rigid framework which interferes with the whole process of creation."

It is through letting go and letting God, while keeping your attention on your INTENTION as having *already* been realized, that you release any need to make something happen. Rather than using your willpower in a struggle to bring something about, you rest in the trust of God that what is for your highest and best good will be realized in the perfect time and space in your life.

In *The Pathway of Roses*, Christian D. Larson writes "We must awaken the spiritual cause before we can secure the physical effect, but it is only through faith that we enter into the world of spiritual cause. Faith produces spiritual unity, and when we are one with the spirit we become conscious of the life, the richness and the power of the spirit. In consequence, we cause that which is in the spirit to be brought forth in the body, because what we gain consciousness of in the within we invariably express in the without."

Faith is the instrument we use to bring ourselves into conscious contact with the spiritual essence—the quality of God—that is behind any physical INTENTION that we have been inspired to claim. Truly, it is the God *quality* of Adventure (or Oneness, or Beauty or Freedom) that is wanting expression through us when we experience the desire to travel. In fact, contained within each of the 64 or more INTENTIONS you have identified on your Mind of the Heart Map is one or more *qualities* of God waiting to move through you.

As we continually practice faith in the Divine Idea of our lives, we align ourselves within the I AM of our being. "Faith is the substance of things hoped for, the evidence of things not seen" (Heb. 11:1). To practice pure faith is to have unshakable belief in the INTENTION and to accept and trust that the idea is not only possible but that it is manifesting at the perfect time for our highest good. Faith is a spiritual conviction that what we **know** has greater power than any apparent material appearance and/or resistance. Thus in faith, we can surrender into the vision of our I AM and know at the deepest level of our being that it is the Father/Mother God within us that does the work. It is through the active practice of faith that we are able to know that our prayers are answered, even before we have uttered them. We affirm that our INTENTIONS are fulfilled and realized without anything more from us than our choice and conscious agreement to allow them to come through us.

Faith alone is required while "waiting upon the Lord" to bring the invisible cause into our world of effects. Here are two very practical action steps of faith that you can take to keep your doubting mind of the mind (ego) happy.

Lowering the Screen of Anxiety

In the face of your as-yet-to-be realized INTENTIONS, your ego may well start to experience fear. Notice how it immediately throws up a screen of anxiety. It thinks it must convince you that you are not worthy of such lofty intentions, or that your dreams are impossible for "it" to achieve. By activating the Principle of Faith, you can use your will power—not to make something happen in the world of effects—but to lower that screen of anxiety. Then you are free to step over it, keeping your attention on your INTENTION. By focusing on your INTENTION, rather than the barriers your ego perceives to be standing in your way, you are keeping yourself open to the field of all possibilities for bringing about your desired outcome.

A student in the *5 GIFTS for an Abundant Life!*™ course utilized this activity of faith in a wondrous way. Robert hadn't said much during the first few weeks, and I got the impression he was a bit overwhelmed by all of the ideas being presented. (Can you relate?) During the "Intention Setting" week he had reluctantly and briefly shared his Mind of the Heart Map, seemingly embarrassed by its simplicity amid the plethora of creative presentations by other students. A lively discussion about *Lowering the Screen of Anxiety* had followed our sharing time, but Robert had appeared baffled by the whole thing. Imagine my surprise when he came into class the following week nearly bursting at the seams with the desire to share his story.

In his late 50s, Robert revealed to the class that he had been unemployed for many months, the human flotsam of yet another corporate merger. He related that each passing income-less month had contributed to his anxiety so that he had begun to feel hopeless about his situation. The media's reports on the local and national economy, as well as the unfavorable hiring statistics for "aging" employees in his field, had morphed Robert's screen of anxiety into a veritable fortress wall.

He shared with us that it was all he could do in his anxious state to try to appear calm and qualified to a potential employer when he was interviewed for a long-awaited and hoped-for job. Then, when he had been selected as one of three finalists for that position, he said he felt reduced to near paralysis.

As he stood in the lobby of the office where the second interview was to take place, the realization hit him: his screen of anxiety was looming larger than life. He recognized that he had unconsciously created a screen that was completely blocking him from manifesting his INTENTION: to get this job, to be paid well and to be able to put his considerable talents to work once again. Flashing on the 5 GIFTS course lesson of consciously lowering the screen of anxiety he decided, "It's now or never!" He visualized that very large screen of anxiety that was standing between him and his INTENTION being lowered slowly to the ground. In his mind's eye he stepped over it and walked into his interview.

He said he'd felt a physical release in his gut at the moment he let go of the worry and stepped into faith. To a standing ovation he told the class that he was beginning his new job in a week and was so looking forward to tithing . . . on an income that was more than he had ever made. *Lowering the Screen of Anxiety* is a faith exercise that lets us release ourselves from the clutches of anxiety, fear and unworthiness and move to a place of unity—with faith in— our INTENTIONS and desires.

Seeing It Right

When the ego knows that it cannot deliver the INTENTIONS that our Mind of the Heart desires, another of its favorite tricks is to try to make them happen, to "fix" the circumstances in the outer world. The mind of the mind only knows how to operate in the material world. It is a complete stranger to the spiritual realm. Therefore, we can know that the ego is running the show when all we want to do is change the circumstances in our lives— perceiving those circumstances as "wrong" and trying to set them "right." We have all experienced this drive to take charge and to set it right when confronted with what appear to be overwhelming obstacles. For example, we get the second job so we can afford that dream trip to Egypt; we go on a severe diet in order to look good and catch the guy/girl of our dreams; we sign up for three concurrent classes in metaphysics to get our spiritual growth mastered in short order. While all of these activities in themselves may ultimately contribute to realizing our dreams, in reality they may well keep us from putting our attention where it really belongs, because we are concentrating on "conditions" rather than *consciousness*. Where our attention belongs is on the INTENTION and our unconditional acceptance of it.

You will remember that having an Abundant Life means having a changed consciousness. This journey into God's vision for our lives is an *inside job*. If we are only pouring our energy out into the world of effects, and not doing the inner work of changing our consciousness to *become* that quality of God that wants to express through us, then we labor in vain. Instead of scurrying around trying to make something happen—"setting it right," we want to keep our attention on our INTENTION. We want to put our energy into seeing and believing that it is manifesting perfectly in our lives—*Seeing It Right*. So, to keep the ego in check and ourselves in balance, simply remember "*Don't set it right, See It Right!*"

Prayer

With the GIFT of INTENTIONS you commit yourself to these Spiritual Principles of consciousness as you move in the direction of realizing the dreams and aspirations you've set down on your Mind of the Heart Map. There's just one last item necessary for your journey into your new life—and perhaps the most important one—*Prayer*. It is *Prayer* that will enfold all the contents of your consciousness, and when used in reverence and with feeling, *Prayer* will be the full expression and the culmination of all the rest.

Once again, let us turn to *The Pathway of Roses* for inspiration from Christian D. Larson: "To pray in the feeling that knows that what we pray for is, even now, ready to be given to us, is to combine the desire for expression with the realization of possession, and we thus comply fully with the law of supply. In this attitude we have faith, and it is only through faith that we can enter into the spirit of that which we desire to actually possess . . . when our prayer for that which we desire is strengthened by the positive faith that we have already received it, we remove all doubts and barriers and enter at once into actual and conscious possession."

Prayer is the path to becoming our INTENTIONS, to manifesting our dreams. It is by praying that we activate the faith in God that allows what It wants to express through us to become our life experience. *Prayer* aligns us with our Higher Self, our deepest inner purpose, our life plan, our Mind of the Heart Map. As we go to God we are knowing and asking—not begging, bargaining and beseeching. (See the Appendix for a discussion of prayer.) Through *Prayer* we strengthen our awareness of Who we are (God Beings), how deserving we are, how sure we are that what we are claiming is for our highest good, how grateful we are that the INTENTION is already ours in the Mind and Heart of God, and how willing we are to let go and let God bring about our heart's desires.

When we pray, knowing and feeling that what we desire is already ours, our consciousness is wrapped in the faith and trust of God, and the seeds of our desires are allowed to grow and flourish. When we pray often, passionately, and in true faith and detachment, we glean the blessings contained within the prayer. We realize that *Prayer* is the power to change consciousness. And a changed consciousness reveals a changed life . . . an Abundant Life!

And so you have the tools to manifesting your INTENTIONS. Let's review them.

- Detach: *Let go and let God!* . . . Simple but not easy.
- Practice faith in the Divine Idea by *Lowering the Screen of Anxiety* and *Seeing It Right* rather than setting it right.
- *Pray!*

Be ready to experience the manifestations that are about to pour forth in your life.

A Mystic Speaks on Manifesting Intentions

Alan Cohen
from *A Deep Breath of Life*

Consciousness, not Conditions

One of the questions I am most frequently asked is, "How do I know if something I am praying for is in my best interest? What if I am imposing my will over God's will? How can I tell if my request is being inspired by love or driven by my ego?"

A rule of thumb that I suggest is to assume that your inspirations are coming from right intuition, and act with authority. Once in a while you will find that you have made a mistake, but in the long run you will be way ahead of where you would be if you assume that your intuitions are guided by ego and do nothing.

The real answer to the question is to understand that what you are seeking is not really conditions, but consciousness. You may be praying for a new BMW, but what you really want is to know that you are an abundant being living in a wealthy universe. You may be seeking a soulmate, but behind your search is the quest to know that you are lovable and cherishable. You may want to have a number-one hit on the pop charts, but behind that desire is the wish to feel acknowledged and important. You can get the conditions, but if you do not have the consciousness, you will be ever seeking and striving for more conditions. If you have the consciousness, however, the conditions will usually manifest automatically, and even if they do not, you will be secure in your wholeness.

If you aren't sure if what you are praying for is correct, complete your prayer with "this or better." Tell God (and remind yourself) that you are doing the best you can with what you know, and if there is something more wonderful available, you are willing to give up your current idea for the bigger picture.

Personal Success Story

A Real Life Moment Of
Manifesting INTENTION

Manifesting in Ease and Grace
by Vivianne Thomas

We learned that we would be creating prayer sticks at the fourth meeting of our *5 GIFTS for an Abundant Life!*™ course. I arrived at class that Monday evening with a stick I'd found on a summer hike in Montana and a small beach rock with a hole through its center. Class began as usual with an opening meditation and a prayer. It was during the meditation that the special intention for my prayer stick came to me—to meet my divine complement. When the meditation ended I wrote my intention down on a slip of paper in the form of a prayer. Then I began to select the rest of the materials I would use for my prayer stick from the two tables piled high with supplies: eucalyptus and oak sticks, raffia, colored yarns, stones, beads of all shapes and sizes, feathers, bells, and more.

To make our prayer sticks we first wrapped our written intention prayer around our chosen sticks and then decorated them however we felt moved to. Throughout this creative process we were in silence, centered in the feeling that our intention had *already* manifested. When we finished the creation process I felt incredibly empowered as I stood in a circle with my 30 other classmates as we passed the prayer sticks from hand to hand, blessing each and every one as it made its way around the circle.

As that week passed, I could literally feel myself being drawn to meet a wonderful man. Sunday was Mother's Day. I'd made plans with a friend to go to the Wild Animal Park outside San Diego, but at the last minute she had to cancel. Something deep inside me said, "Go anyway. Celebrate Mother's Day with all the beautiful animal moms."

I was at the Park when it opened, and my inner voice immediately sent me to "Condor Hill," an area I'd never visited before. Within a few minutes of my arrival, I saw a nice looking man walking along by himself. We smiled at each other and said "hello." Then he continued on his way. I moseyed around for a while and then walked down the backside of the hill. When I'd almost reached the bottom, I saw him again. He was seated on a bench. As I got closer his face lit up and he wished me a Happy Mother's Day. And the next thing I knew I was sitting beside him and we were laughing and talking as if we'd known each other for years.

We spent many delightful hours together over the next six weeks. From the very first, our relationship was one of complete openness and safety, to a degree that I had never before experienced with a man. Although I was disappointed when we made a mutual decision to go our separate ways, I relish and am so grateful for everything I received from beginning to end. Now I know what is truly possible in a love relationship, and I understand the power of my own intention to create what I want in my life.

———— ❀ ————

Give Your Gift PRACTICE

Heart Opening Instructions
for
Manifesting INTENTIONS

To Pray is To Know

*"Wherever two or more are gathered together in My name,
I am there in the midst of them." (Matthew 18:20)*

Call your Prosperity Prayer Partner to share this exercise. Together, bring before you the Mind of Your Heart Maps. Holding your maps, review all of your divinely inspired INTENTIONS written there. Now, take five to ten minutes to close your eyes and go into the silence. During this brief meditation, just allow the INTENTIONS that came to you through Divine intuition and inspiration to surface. Notice, too, any thoughts that may be less than supportive of your owning and claiming God's idea of your life. Out of the bouquet of your dreams and desires, choose one INTENTION that you intuitively feel most strongly wants to bloom and blossom. Take a moment to immerse yourself in this INTENTION. Feel it. See it. Hear it. Smell it. Taste it. Allow yourself to fully own that quality of God, and the experience of that quality of God. Feel that INTENTION as already manifested into your life. Science tells us that the mind doesn't know the difference between that which is vividly visualized and that which is actually seen.

As you emerge from this sacred and meditative space, fully in the feeling tone of living in your already manifested INTENTION, set that manifestation into further motion by creating a

66

prayer for it. The following format will assist you in developing an affirmative prayer for you and your Prosperity Prayer Partner to use together and alone. Please note that your Prosperity Prayer Partner's response comes in the middle of your prayer and can be omitted when you are praying for yourself. However, be aware how powerful it is for you to affirm the truth for one another by praying together on a daily basis.

Prayer for the Manifestation of My Intention

"I know that God is everywhere present as Love and the Source of All Good. Within the Omnipresence of God, I know I AM a radiant expression of the Divine Source, as I also know this for my Prosperity Prayer Partner. I AM (*We ARE*) One in That which is holy and pure Abundance.

I now know and claim that I AM (living, experiencing, expressing, embodying)_____."

[fill in the blank with your INTENTION, i.e. $xxx,xxx annual income; my true life partner; travel to India; a deeper meditation practice, etc.]

Prosperity Prayer Partner's Response:

"I know that you are_____NOW!"

[S/he repeats your INTENTION back to you.]

"I AM thankful to know the truth. And I am grateful to know Who I AM: a loving, glorious being of God. I surrender this prayer into the heart of God and allow it to be. Amen."

Follow your intuition and respond by changing and/or adding other INTENTIONS from your Mind of the Heart Map whenever you feel inspired to do so.

Prayer is the power that changes consciousness. Pray and watch your life become an Abundant Life!

ACKNOWLEDGE YOURSELF

Giving the GIFT of
Manifesting INTENTIONS to You!

Create or buy a surprise gift for your Prosperity Prayer Partner to honor and thank her/him for all the contributions made to your Abundant Life!

CHAPTER 5

FORGIVENESS
of Others

Give Away

*I*t's the largest of the 5 GIFTS left by the mysterious Stranger that day. It appears there are two boxes inside this butter-yellow, sunflower-print gift bag. You reach for the card attached to the handles and read the message it contains:

FORGIVENESS
of
SELF AND OTHERS

Through Giving These GIFTS
You Are Set Free!

Accompanying the card are "General Operating Instructions" for the whole spiritual practice of FORGIVENESS. They state that whether you are practicing FORGIVENESS for yourself or another, these definitions and principles apply. And so you sit down to read, before you begin unwrapping the two boxes.

GENERAL OPERATING INSTRUCTIONS:
FORGIVENESS

FORGIVENESS is a spiritual practice, not a mental one. When we try to forgive from the mind we end up in a battle of righteousness and separation from the one(s) we are seeking to forgive. On its own, the mind will argue for revenge, try to prove itself right, and swiftly assume the role of judge and jury. In the spiritual practice of forgiving there is no ego, and the wrongs that were done to us lose their sting because condemning thoughts and judgments are transcended. We are connecting soul to soul with the self, an individual or a group, thereby acknowledging the Spirit, the God presence within each. The spiritual being knows only Acceptance, Oneness, Joy and Love. S/He seeks to love unconditionally and wants nothing but a loving relationship with the Divine in and through all of Its creation.

FORGIVENESS frees the forgiver. The result of unforgivingness is the very thing you don't want—the binding of yourself to the person or situation you are judging or condemning. In the name of righteousness and expectations left unfulfilled, you move down life's path amassing resentments, anger, guilt, regrets and shame that you drag along behind you like a sack of stones. The burden of these emotions, sustained by not forgiving, becomes heavier and heavier, as you add rock after rock.

Eventually you become so buried under the weight of your reactions to the hurts and wrongs you have experienced (including the self-inflicted ones) that you are paralyzed by the very thing you had wanted to be separated from! Stuck in the past—whether you are conscious of it or not—you fracture yourself and miss the glory of **now**. You are not able to be fully present. Your energy is tied up under the burden of attachment to whatever it was that didn't meet your expectations. There is simply less of you available in the present to enjoy your health, relationships, creative work, or abundant finances.

FORGIVENESS frees the forgiver. Stop to think about it. . . . The only reason why there is anything to forgive in the first place is that someone or something didn't do what **you** expected, and you decided they should pay for it! When you finally become sick and tired of being sick and tired of being a victim and jailed by the past, it is time to move into the spiritual practice of forgiving.

The reason to forgive is to claim your own freedom, not because you want to let anyone "off the hook." When the question is "Would you rather be happy, free and loving . . . than right?" let your answer be a resounding "Yes!"

FORGIVENESS is terribly misunderstood. As a mental exercise, forgiveness can be construed as giving in to someone's inappropriate actions, condoning their behavior, even giving permission for that behavior to be done again . . . in other words, a big sign of weakness. FORGIVENESS has often been erroneously identified with the thought and feeling tone of *turning the other cheek*. When forgiving is done from the mind instead of from the heart it is nothing more than a spiritual bypass. In the name of doing the right thing, such as "getting over it" or being "the first to apologize," we fail to honor the real feelings that we have. By not acknowledging our natural human reactions—be they emotions of rage, hurt, shame or any other feelings—we dishonor ourselves. It's no wonder that many people have considered forgiving to be a very unappealing, even demeaning, process!

It is essential that we understand forgiving as the spiritual practice that it is. Coming from the Mind of the Heart—rather than the mind of the mind—the practice is *For Giving*, the giving of Compassion, Understanding and Unconditional Love to self and others.

It is also important to note here that FORGIVENESS is our job, not God's. In truth, God knows only Itself (Good) and realizes **all** as perfect. It is the "humanhood" of us that, through the gift of will, can use that will to see ourselves as separate from one another and God. It is the humanhood of us that lives from judgment, condemnation, and duality (good/bad and right/wrong) and therefore needs forgiveness. God as pure Love has no reason to forgive. We as humans must forgive ourselves and one another.

Another myth about FORGIVENESS is that it is a one-time event, and, once done, never has to be revisited. In most instances, that myth couldn't be further from the truth. Forgiveness is a process that may take years of intention and focus to complete. When asked by the Apostle Peter, "How many times do I need to forgive, Lord . . . up to seven times?" Jesus responded, "I do not say to you, up to seven times, but up to seventy times seven" (Matt. 18:21,22). In other words, do it until it's done. FORGIVENESS is complete and finished when there is an abounding, heart-opening feeling of GRATITUDE for the person, event, and/or self. (Not surprisingly, GRATITUDE is the first of the 5 GIFTS.)

FORGIVENESS is mastery . . . a practice. The rules for forgiving are designed for the Mind of the Heart (our spiritual nature) and must be followed from there, even though our pain or other emotions are rooted in the mind of our minds.

- In forgiving, we look to Spirit in each person and forgive them without expecting them to change.
- There are no strings attached in FORGIVENESS work. Our intention is to release and let go of the feeling of hurt, while at the same time wanting nothing from the other person, so that we can be free. We realize this may take years and we invoke the qualities of patience and loving kindness toward ourselves during the process.
- We do not "forgive and forget." We **want** to remember

so that we can assure ourselves that what happened won't happen again.

- There is no spiritual bypass in FORGIVENESS. If we have feelings of rage and thoughts of revenge, we have to process them. There is little hope for authentic, complete FORGIVENESS without taking care of our human/emotional being. That is, we are not allowed to use concepts of God or being holy and self-sacrificing as excuses to gloss over our feelings of pain and hurt. Not only is this true for our emotional selves but also for our physical selves. If action needs to be taken (e.g., reports to authorities, protection measures, etc.) we must honor ourselves and do what we are guided to do.

- If we are stuck and cannot find it in our hearts to forgive, let us be willing to be willing to be willing to forgive. From that place, we can consciously create an opening through which we can invoke the Divine within us and surrender to it. With a softening and an opening in our hearts through this letting go, we can allow the Divine within us to lead the way. In doing this we are aware that the Christ/Buddha presence within us can and does see ONLY the Christ/Buddha within the other. We will forgive 70 x 7 times—for as long as it takes.

- We take responsibility for our part in the situation whether we are wronged or the wrongdoer, releasing any idea of having been victimized or having been the victimizer. In the spiritual realm, there are no victims, only holy ones, God Beings.

- We can and do realize that by being the giver of the Love of God we are lifted out of the emotional prison of unforgivingness and moved to the plane of Truth where we are the beholders of the Love of God in the other,

thus freeing both of us into our greatest yet to be.

FORGIVENESS is complete when you live in GRATITUDE for the whole experience. GRATITUDE is the last chapter in the FORGIVENESS process. It is by being grateful to the other for the experience that you know you have released the burden and all attachments. From that place of gratefulness you can see the gifts you have gleaned from the other person, the path that has led you to love yourself more fully, the perfection of your soul's life pattern. With a grateful heart, you can live in freedom **as** the Abundance of God.

Giving the GIFT OF FORGIVENESS sets us free. THANK YOU, GOD!

As intrigued as you've ever been, you remove the first of the two packages from the gift sack. It's wrapped in kiddy birthday paper—dancing blue giraffes and pink elephants. Why would this whimsical present be included with the ones the Stranger left for you? The tag lies beneath the bushy multi-colored bow. It reads FORGIVENESS of OTHERS. How bizarre! "Why would such a serious gift be wrapped like this?" you wonder. You tear off the wrapping paper, and as soon as you open the box a familiar little voice emerges. It's a voice that you immediately recognize, and it's telling you that it is the voice of your Inner Child.

"I am hurting! I need you to listen to me. I need you to understand what happened to me. And I need you to love me no matter what—even when I tell you how mad I am at you because you haven't been paying attention to me. . . . Don't you understand? You think that I'll go away when you ignore me, but I won't. I can't go away because I am a part of you. I'm the part of you that holds childhood memories and old pain. And you have to pay attention to me . . . you have to love and support me so that we can, together, get past the hurt and the feelings I could never

*express. **Only when you love me unconditionally can we for-***
give!"

For a moment you sit there in stunned silence. You certainly weren't
expecting a powerful little voice to come out of that present, but you can
feel the resonance of what you've just heard. You know that it has never
worked to ignore your Inner Child, but you don't understand how listen-
ing to the voice of your child prepares you for the FORGIVENESS of
OTHERS. . . .

There is a wounded, disowned aspect of all of us. This "little
self" has been given many names: ego, ego mind, humanity, inner
child. Here it will be known simply as *the kid*. In all likelihood,
your kid has been silenced and abused for eons. You believed the
criticisms and admonitions of your parents and other authority
figures. You were criticized for your looks ("Oh honey, your fore-
head is just too high!"), your coordination ("You run like you have
two left feet!"), your way of thinking ("Where did you ever get
that idea?"), your emotional responses ("Big boys don't cry!"), and
your need to belong ("Children should be seen but not heard."").
You decided that it wasn't safe to be who you were and that you
could not get the love you desperately wanted if you allowed your
natural self to be present. Like all of us, at some point in your
early life you made the decision that your kid needed to be
repressed, so you stopped being you.

As time went by you really came to believe that you had
done away with the kid. But the truth is that the kid didn't go
away, you just became unconscious of it . . . even while it has continued to act like an emotional, love-starved four-to seven-year-
old who has been running your life.

Not willing to be shut down, your kid has been doing end-
runs around you to get that love from other sources that it can
truly only be satisfied by getting from you. Left in its wake are
your addictions, your destructive and abusive relationships, your

pain from betrayal and abandonment. Able to communicate only through emotions, your kid brandishes drama as a weapon to get your attention. Its greatest voice up until now has been your seemingly unexplained or groundless rages and sometimes overwhelming waves of sadness.

What you hold in your hands—the Voice of your Kid—is the sickle that clears your path to the FORGIVENESS of others. By allowing your kid (in the Heart Opener practice near the end of this chapter) to express the feelings that have been repressed up until now, you are setting in motion the integration process that is essential for FORGIVENESS. When you can accept, acknowledge and unconditionally love your kid and the unexpressed and repressed feelings that have kept you in the prison of the past, you are ready to forgive those who appear to have harmed you . . . to let them and you out of the jail you have created in your heart. What a GIFT!

A Mystic Speaks on Forgiveness of Others

Meredith L. Young-Sowers
from *Angelic Messenger Cards*

Love is the emotional and spiritual energy
that ties you
to those who have hurt you.
The issues that seem to defy forgiveness
are always aligned in some way with love:
the love you never received,
the love that you offered
and others rejected or betrayed,
the love that was used
to manipulate or control you.
Love is the basis of your life's well-being,
but in tying your spiritual energy reserves to old hurts
you are severely limiting the energy of love
available to you in the present moment.
Perhaps this is the time
to search your heart
for those you still need to forgive more fully.

A Real Life Moment Of
FORGIVENESS of Others

Forgiveness: A Door To a Brighter World
by Riti Di Angeli

Forgiveness—like a magic wand—opened a gate in my heart. The love trapped inside broke free and dissolved the chains of resentment and fear that kept me in bondage for thirteen years, following the end of a turbulent marriage. Anyone who has seen the film "Sleeping With The Enemy" with Julia Roberts, a film about a battered woman who escaped from a jealous, violent, abusive husband, would understand the kind of married life K and I had together.

After we got married, I expected him to be a loving and considerate husband, especially because I was pregnant. Instead, after our "first night," K stated clearly that he was my husband, the only boss in the house, and my role as a wife was to obey him and serve him without questioning. Our home became a battleground. When we argued he became violent; he beat me. I was miserable and craved love and peace.

I left the battleground after our daughter was born. The last words I heard from K were, "I'll kidnap your daughter and you'll never see her again in your life!" I took his threat seriously because he had been kidnapped at age four by his own father and moved from school to school throughout the country to prevent

80

his mother from finding him. He did not see his mother again until he was 20.

I feared K would take revenge because I had dared to leave him. Some nights a freezing current ran along my spine and woke me up. I ran to my daughter's room to see if she was safe. Then flashes of resentment would clamp down on my heart; I could not stand the idea of seeing him again. When he stopped paying child support, I did not take him to court because I wanted him out my life.

Though he vanished from our lives, he didn't vanish from my mind. I was haunted by fearful thoughts about the safety of my daughter. Fortunately, I was able to prevent my anxiety from bleeding through to her and jeopardizing her right to feel safe in the world. I strove not to become an overprotective or possessive mother. I wanted my daughter to be independent and fearless . . . to try her own wings and fly. She began to practice "independence" at age five when I allowed her to go by herself to a nearby store to buy candy.

The store was right in front of the apartment building where we lived. Every time she went to that store I was afraid she would be kidnapped. I ran toward a window in the upper floor and stared at the street. I watched her crossing the street and entering the store. My heart pounded fast and my stomach contracted. I wouldn't calm down until she came back. For three years I stared at that street and watched my daughter every time she went to the store. Not until she was eight was I able to experience relief from my anxiety over her. At that time I remarried and we moved to another city.

Having a man in the house put a halt to my fear. My husband was a thick wall around me that would prevent K from kidnapping my daughter. My fear diminished, but my feelings of resentment and hate did not. If anyone mentioned his name my stomach tied up in a knot. I feared the idea that one day he would reappear in my life.

After 13 years of not hearing from K, I was forced to write him a letter asking him to pay child support. Since our divorce, my second husband had been providing for his own children and also for K's and my daughter. He said that was not fair so I had to ask K to send money for his daughter. Reluctantly, I sent him a letter hoping he would never answer it. When six months passed and K had given no sign of even being alive, I felt relieved. I still feared him and I couldn't forgive him. I was full of resentment.

One night while studying *Science and Health with Key to the Scripture*, the Christian Science textbook, I understood that I needed to stop hating K if I wanted to be free from the chains of fear and resentment, which had kept me in bondage for 13 years. I was learning that "Man," created by God in His own image and likeness, was the Christ, the sum or incorporation of God's spiritual qualities and ideas. Only through seeing K as the Christ would I be released from resentment and fear. I was determined to forgive K, but I could not do it by myself. I needed help.

I closed my eyes and asked God to help me see the Christ-like qualities in K. I pondered about the qualities I had seen in K when we first met. He was gentle, honest, independent, self-confident and a hard worker. I pictured K on the screen of my mind and I asked God to show me K as He saw him. Immediately a shimmering light came from K's chest. As the light grew brighter and brighter, the human form disappeared behind the light. My heart opened as a wave of love came through and embraced K and me as one. I loved him. It was so easy for me to love the Christ. Then I fell asleep with light in my mind and love in my heart.

I woke up the next morning freed from resentment. I was no

longer afraid of K. I had forgotten why I had hated him so much. I was completely free from the tyranny of fear and hatred that had enslaved me for years! That very day at noon K called me and said he had received my letter and would send money for his daughter every month. Eventually he met his daughter and they became friends.

When K and I were together he was an atheist. He did not believe in life after death, and he forbade me to read metaphysics and talk about spirituality. Now K believes in God, meditates, and is on a spiritual path. We talk about metaphysics when we meet; we speak the same language. Did he change after my forgiveness? No. He was and still is the same man. When I saw him as he really was, I set him free from the role he played for me to learn that forgiveness is the way to have freedom and peace of mind.

I am so thankful now to K for that powerful lesson in forgiveness that brought me happiness and peace at last. Because I was able to forgive my worst enemy, it became easier for me to forgive others. Having had the opportunity to share my forgiveness story in the *5 GIFTS* course has only served to validate how this powerful process can be a gift that keeps on giving. The daily practice of forgiveness has enriched all of my relationships. Forgiveness freed my mind from resentment, opened it to a brighter world, and continues to bless my life in so many ways.

Give Your Gift PRACTICE

Heart Opening Instructions
for
FORGIVENESS of Others

Forgiveness Letter

To further the expression of your kid's voice, it helps to explore the repressed emotions attached to an unforgiven person in your life. The following journaling exercise is designed for this purpose as it leads you down the FORGIVENESS path. Remember to use all of the prompts beneath each stated feeling, beginning at number one, *ANGER*. No matter how irrational or brutally honest it may sound, allow the voice of your Inner Child to express itself in depth . . . even if you think you are "over" all of those feelings by now.

Do not be surprised if you are unable on the fifth step of the letter to reach a feeling tone of love or FORGIVENESS on the first try. Pay particular attention to the *FEAR* section for insights as to *why* you/your kid has held on to being unforgiving. Feel free to use this writing exercise for any person, institution, circumstance—and, yes, even God—for whom you may hold unforgiving attachments. It is recommended that you begin at the beginning, with your parents or childhood caregivers.

FORGIVENESS LETTER

Dear_____,   Date_____

I am writing you to share my feelings.

1. ANGER

I am angry that _____

I feel frustrated _____

I don't like it _____

I feel really annoyed _____

I want _____

2. SADNESS

I feel disappointed _____

I am sad that _____

I feel so hurt _____

I wanted _____

I want _____

3. FEAR

I feel worried _____

I am afraid _____

I feel so scared _____

I do not want _____

I need _____

I want _____

4. REGRET

I feel embarrassed _____

I am so sorry _____

I feel ashamed _____

I didn't want _____

I want _____

5. FORGIVENESS & LOVE

I forgive you for _____

I love _____

I appreciate _____

I am grateful for _____

I understand _____

I know _____

Love,

_____

Now read the letter aloud to yourself. Pay attention to what you have said and allow yourself to feel all of the feelings you've expressed . . . as well as the ones that lie "between the lines."

You know that you have plumbed the depths of your kid's feelings when s/he reaches a feeling of FORGIVENESS and Love. Once you feel complete with this part of the Heart Opener, do the second part of the exercise. In this part you will write a *FORGIVENESS Response Letter* back to yourself and your kid from the person to whom you have written the *FORGIVENESS Letter*. Include in this response all those things you have ever wanted to hear from that person. Be sure to stay out of your head when writing this response—come from your heart (and theirs!). Be willing to be surprised by what comes back to you in this letter.

Once you've completed both of these letters, make a special date to sit down with your Prosperity Prayer Partner. Say an opening prayer to create a loving space. Then read them your *FORGIVENESS Letter*. Next, have your partner read your *FORGIVENESS Response Letter* back to you. This is powerful!

FORGIVENESS RESPONSE LETTER

Date _____

Dear (Your Name), _____

    I am writing to share my response to your letter _____

    I am so grateful to you for sharing your feelings _____

    I understand _____

    I am so sorry _____

    I was afraid _____

    I didn't know _____

    I want you to know_____

    I appreciate _____

    I love _____

Love,

_____

ACKNOWLEDGE YOURSELF

Giving the GIFT of FREEDOM THROUGH FORGIVENESS to You!

Ask your kid what s/he would like for being so loving and forgiving to those you have released in the name of your freedom and abundance. In my *Loving the Kid Within* classes, these are some of the things that others have done that may inspire you.

- Write a Love Letter to your kid.
- Take a romp through her/his favorite toy store.
- Let your kid pick out a journal and pen that you two can use to communicate with each other.
- Get out the paper, scissors, glitter-glue and colored pens, then let her/him create!

If you ask, your Inner Child will let you know what s/he wants. Take the time to give your kid that gift today. Giving to yourself is the greatest gift you can give!

CHAPTER 6

Self FORGIVENESS

Give Up

You remember that there's one more surprise waiting for you inside the forgiveness gift bag. You reach into the bag and feel something down at the very bottom. It's a flat, thin, square package that is instantly recognizable as a CD. You unwrap it and read the title: Self FORGIVENESS. Opening the plastic case you pull out the cover insert. With the insert in hand you grab your cup, settle into your comfy chair and read these words:

> ### If there were no judgements, there would be Nothing to FORGIVE . . .

Immediately you think about the voices of self-judgment inside of you—the ones that communicate in many tones, all of them critical. Taking a sip of your favorite brew, you exclaim to yourself, "Here we go!"

Self FORGIVENESS is essential for an Abundant Life. In my years of counseling I have recognized that our critical inner voices are a compilation of the voices of others—the opinions and judgments of parents, teachers, and all other authority figures that we feared as children. I call this strident chorus "The Committee." Relentless in its self-appointed job, it holds us in some measure of guilt, doubt or fear about the decisions and actions we have taken throughout our lives. The Committee keeps logs of our past "wrongs" in a carefully organized Book of Evidence, ready to use against us at any and every moment.

The Committee's job is to convince us that we **are** our mistakes. Like the prosecution team that is successful at getting only damning evidence admitted, The Committee mounts and remounts the evidence until its victory is assured. It uses our mistakes, weaknesses, foibles and errors to convict us; it uses concurrent lifetime sentences of shame, blame, guilt and resentment to imprison us; and it uses an isolated, locked-down cell of fear to keep us from breaking out and claiming our freedom. Under these conditions we dare not see ourselves as the innocent, loving Beings of God whose Divine Nature knows no wrong.

Reminded of The Committee, you can feel the tremendous burden that your self-judgments have become. Like those you have leveled against others, these self-judgments have accumulated into a heavy weight that you drag with you wherever you go . . . the Jailer and the Jailed.

In order to be free and abundant, we must lay these burdens of self-judgment down. Just as we recognized that we had to forgive others when the burdens of guilt, anger, resentments, and shame became too much, here too we must make room for Self FORGIVENESS. In order to experience the freedom and abundance that are our natural state of being, we must receive and give to ourselves the GIFT of Self FORGIVENESS.

In spite of all the experience you have had being your own worst critic, there is a radical yet simple step-by-step approach that can be taken to free yourself from the jail of self-condemnation. The first step is to banish any denial that you might have about the mistakes you've made. Denial is simply our automatic, defensive response to self-judgment. Denial and self-judgment are the powerful partners in a self-perpetuating cycle of disclaiming responsibility. If the mistakes you have been judging yourself for are true, admit to them. Consciously claim them, but this time without the added "charge" of judgment.

The second step in Self FORGIVENESS is opening to the deeper truth. As you claim each mistake and drop the judgment you have held around it, you separate *yourself* from it. You realize that you—you as God Being—are not it. You are not that or any other mistake you have made. Yet, by owning your actions, you can move into a place where you take responsibility for them.

In the third step you give yourself the opportunity to do something about the mistakes you have made, bringing closure to them at last. Once you have admitted the transgression to yourself, you can consider telling someone else . . . a person you trust, such as your Prosperity Prayer Partner. I have found that by admitting a mistake to another person (a therapist, counselor, spiritual practitioner) the very act of disclosure takes my intense feelings of guilt, shame and anger away. By telling my story to a trusted prayer partner or colleague, the burden is somehow lessened . . . and I am more willing to accept and love myself.

The fourth step is to make amends to the person you have harmed or hurt, if at all possible. You will be guided to perform the action that serves you and the other person, if you come from the Mind of your Heart. However, if The Committee is left in charge, you may find yourself resisting this step, or worse, attempting to use "being sorry" as a way to manipulate the person you've wronged, or even to make yourself look good.

Once you have completed these Self FORGIVENESS steps, you are ready to proceed to the Heart Openers at the end of this chapter. The same caveat holds true for Self FORGIVENESS as for other FORGIVENESS work: it takes practice. This means that rarely does the first round complete the intention to forgive. Rather, we are to practice FORGIVENESS "seventy times seven" until we reach our goal, and the only feeling we are experiencing is GRATITUDE.

A Mystic Speaks on Self Forgiveness

Paul Ferrini
from *The Twelve Steps of Forgiveness*

The Four Axioms of Forgiveness

1. *Forgiveness starts in our own hearts. Only when we have forgiven ourselves can we give it to or receive it from others.*

2. *Forgiveness is not conditional, even though our practice of it often is.*

3. *Forgiveness is an ongoing process. It continues in response to every judgment we make about ourselves. . . .*

4. *Every gesture of forgiveness is sufficient. Whatever we are able to do now is enough. This understanding enables us to practice forgiveness with forgiveness.*

Personal Success Story

A Real Life Moment Of
Self FORGIVENESS

The Grace of Self Forgiveness
by Rev. Diane Harmony

Our hearts melted into one another's in instant recognition during that first hug. Two bodies reunited after 36 years . . . two spirits that had never been separated. The gap of time was instantly filled during that one moment of reunion. The bond of mother and daughter can never be broken. Only shame, guilt and remorse fed the fire of apparent separation. Only forgiveness would douse the flames and complete the circle of love.

Thirty-six years before, I had given birth to my first daughter and then released her for adoption. Suffering from a heart broken by the decision to honor my parents' wishes that I not marry my first love, I emerged from being an "unwed mother" with emotional scars so great that my only defense was to bury them deeply, pick up my life as though nothing had happened, and go on. So successful was my denial of the gaping hole in my heart that, as the years passed, I could not even remember my child's birth date.

How was it possible then, some 30 years, four children and two marriages later, that I could find myself in a class of spiritual counseling students that had six other women who shared the same closely held past that I did? We were all birth mothers. Our secret became our magnet, and we began to meet and vision a ministry at our church that could prayerfully support all people who are affected by adoption: adoptees, birthparents and adoptive parents. It was a noble idea, and one requiring that we do our own healing work in order to be available to others.

And so we began the excruciating journey of dredging up our pain. We individually faced our own demons—guilt, shame, blame, anger and self-recrimination—at whatever pace we felt capable of moving, and collectively we prayed for one another and all those whose pain we share. We created the Adoption Triad Ministry at the Agape Center of Truth in Los Angeles and invited people touched by adoption to come and tell their stories and join in prayer each month. We opened the way to allow each member of the triad—adoptee, adoptive parent and birth parent—to dialog with the other, seeking an understanding of the unique emotional issues that each carries. And some of us searched for our child and/or parent. My decision to try to find my daughter opened up my personal Pandora's box.

It was in that atmosphere of prayer and spiritual guidance that I felt safe enough to face my own walls of defense and denial and take the steps to bring them down. The process was agonizing. Not only was I delving into the shame and pain I had caused my parents and siblings by becoming a pregnant teenager, I was allowing to surface the hatred I held for myself for not having fought for what I wanted . . . my mate and my baby.

What I was inviting into conscious awareness—and ultimately acceptance—were the shame and guilt of having sinned, according to the church of my childhood as well as the mores of society in 1961. I was admitting that I was filled with rage at my parents for interrupting my fantasy to have the perfect family, and at my boyfriend for not having fought harder to save me from this torturous sentence of a banished offender. During the search for my daughter, I was required on numerous occasions to recall those difficult circumstances surrounding her birth, and it was all I could do to keep from passing out. As I unleashed one tidal wave after another of suppressed feelings, I was constantly on the verge of emotional overwhelm. What kept me going was my deep, deep desire to find my daughter, to tell her how much I loved her, to share with her that she was conceived in love, and to complete the circle that began with her birth.

And so I searched . . . and I prayed . . . and I began to forgive. As I progressed through the classes in spirituality that were preparing me to be a spiritual counselor and prayer practitioner, I came to realize that without forgiveness I would be unable to free myself from the maze of negative self-judgment which I had allowed to tarnish the beauty of the birth of my daughter. I understood that if I were to welcome her with true open arms now, I had to find the *good* in my being her birth mother. I knew that the healing I so dearly sought was possible only when I released my guilt, shame and blame about the circumstances surrounding her coming into this world.

"Seventy times seven." Jesus admonishes us that this is how often we need to forgive in order to be free—in other words, as often as it takes. I was well on my way to completing my forgiveness of the other actors in my drama—my parents, my first love, my church, my society. Now it was time to forgive myself. I had held myself on the cross of self-blame and shame for so long that I wasn't sure how to let myself off.

I began by feeling great compassion for the teenager I was who was so in love and so passionate about life, and who only wanted to experience and express that love in any way she knew how. I listened to that 19-year-old's pain of profound loss and of feeling that she did not belong. That pain had been so severe that she had essentially shut herself off from trusting her own beautiful heart. I listened to her, consoled her, told her how much I loved her and that I would not let that kind of pain happen to her again. The I AM of me (my God Self) forgave her for any belief she held about being a "bad girl," a "sinner," an "undesirable good-for-nothing," and a "cause of pain to others."

The months—and yes, years—that I have spent forgiving the layers of self-recrimination and loathing I felt for myself have truly unburdened me. Freeing myself from the shackles of that seemingly unforgivable and unforgiving past has truly given me a new life. The attitude I now hold toward myself, my family, my first love and my pregnancy is only *gratitude*, gratitude for one of the greatest growth experiences of my life. By coming to terms with my past, the gift of compassion was ignited in me—a gift I can and do readily share with all those I teach and counsel. The reward for my commitment to forgiveness is the profound love I share with my first-born daughter, a love activated the moment we hugged that has continued to enrich my life ever since.

Give Your Gift *PRACTICE*

Heart Opening Instructions
for
Self FORGIVENESS

Self Forgiveness Inventory

From a meditative, non-judgmental, self-loving place, complete the following sentence:
I forgive myself for *judging* myself as

_____

As you scan your life history, list as many entries as you can. For this exercise **do** listen to the voices of The Committee and record the evidence they've been holding against you. Be an investigator here: Impartially search the halls of your mind for the beliefs you have about your being "bad." Dig deep. Stay aware that these are judgments and beliefs about you, not the truth of your Divine Being.

After you have created your inventory list in response to the above statement, complete the exercise by writing: **I forgive myself for temporarily believing in the illusion that I AM separate from God.**

You can now proceed to the Guided Meditation. Bring into this second Heart Opener some of the entries you have listed above, places where you want to practice the Gift of Self FORGIVENESS.

Self Forgiveness Meditation
(To be read to you by another or recorded in your voice for you to listen to. Do not read or record the words in brackets [ ]. These are "stage directions.")

Allow yourself to get comfortable in your favorite place of softness and safety. Feel yourself supported by the surface on which your body is resting, so that you have no need to hold up any part of it. Know that you are supported, as you invite a feeling of nurturing and love to come into your awareness. Gently close your eyes and begin to focus your attention inward. Now . . . draw in one . . . long, deep breath that seems to come from the very depths of your being. And then . . . release the breath in one . . . long . . . sigh. AHHHHHH. Let go of anything that may seem to be holding you back . . . anything that seems to prevent you from relaxing. Take another breath, only this time, let it come from a place even deeper than the last one. . . . As you silently exhale, feel your body releasing even more, immersing itself in a feeling of warmth.

Know you are safe and sound and that all is well. Continue to focus on your breath, breathing in long inhalations and exhalations from the core of your being, allowing your body to go into deeper and deeper relaxation. Notice yourself beginning to let go and surrender to that warm feeling of peace. Let this blanket of relaxation spread over your body and feel your mind becoming calm and peaceful. With your next inhalation, visualize yourself inhaling light. . . . As you exhale imagine you are letting go of all tensions and worries, and allow yourself to totally surrender into the light. For this is a meditation of surrendering to the light of God within you, the Divine Presence. [*Pause* . . . .]

As you continue to visualize and feel this light permeating your being, say to yourself over and over again, "I open myself to receive and accept the transforming light, this Divine Presence, fully into my being." [*Pause* . . . .]

And now shift your attention to the area around your heart and imagine that beautiful light bathing your heart in love and rest. As the light begins to massage that wonderful organ, feel your heart beginning to soften and open. [*Pause* . . . .]

Self FORGIVENESS is an act of the Heart . . . a process of surrendering the heavy burdens of pain, anger and resentment that you feel for yourself, which can cause your heart to shut you out of the Divine Love found there. Realizing that forgiveness is a process and a practice to allow you to return to your awareness of yourself as a Child of God, you enter the remainder of this meditation by being willing to let go of the judgments and condemning thoughts you have of yourself and that keep you out of your own heart. You allow yourself now to totally surrender to the light, as you feel your heart opening in response to the massaging luminescence surrounding it. [*Pause* . . . .]

Imagine yourself now entering your heart on a beam of the beautiful light. You are immediately filled with a feeling of the Presence of Unconditional Love within your own heart. Your attention is drawn to a translucent form seeming to be made up of the light of your own heart, coming to greet you. Drifting to an even deeper state of serenity and calmness, you realize this Radiant Being is the vision of your Holy Self, come to welcome and support you. As you look into the eyes of this being, you feel Love so pure and holy that any residue of fear or separation melts away in the light of that Love. . . . You find yourself . . . immersed . . . in the Presence of Divinity and you feel your Oneness in God.

Your Holy Self holds you and surrounds you, as you move toward the deep center of your heart. There you discover a fire burning on a sacred altar. Next to the translucent steps leading up to that pyre lie the burdens of your past that you are willing to forgive. Shaped like heavy, wooden blocks, they are piled up and waiting for you to carry each one up to the purifying flames burning upon your personal altar.

Bathed in the energy of light and love from your Holy Self,

you approach the pile of blocks, affirming to yourself, "There is only the Love and the Light of God here." You pick up a block . . . a heavy burden of judgment and self-condemnation. You are determined to embrace the full weight of this burden . . . to feel all the feelings of pain and resentment contained within that burden of unforgivingness toward yourself. . . . You open yourself to receive the Gift of Wisdom it has to give you. . . . You allow yourself to be directed to the aspect of yourself that you **know** you are to love and accept before you can fully release this block. [*Pause . . . .*]

You realize that the block is becoming lighter now. . . . As you ascend the steps, you feel that sense of lightness within you. At the top step, you release the wooden burden into the flames of the altar of your heart, and you say to yourself: "I bless myself. . . . I love myself. . . . I forgive myself."

As the flames of your heart engulf the block you say to yourself: "I allow the Love of God within me to consume this burden and the power I have given it. And I am Free. Thank you God." [*Pause . . . .*]

Descending the stairs your being feels noticeably lighter, your heart's light a little brighter. Approaching the pile of burdens you choose another. You strain to pick it up, and once again open to the Wisdom Gift it has for you. You embrace that gift. . . . Allow yourself to visualize and feel all the hurt caused to yourself and others through the action or inaction you committed here . . . and once again be directed to the place within you where you must feel self-compassion and self-acceptance. . . . Aware of your Holy Self, radiating its Love and Light, you ascend the pearly steps and release this burden into the fire of your heart.

As you deposit it into the flames of your altar you say to yourself, "I bless myself. . . . I love myself. . . . I forgive myself." The flames of your heart hungrily engulf the block as you repeat to yourself, "I allow the Love of God within me to consume this burden, and the power I have given it. And I am Free. Thank you God." [*Pause* . . . .]

And now I'll be silent for a time so that you can repeat this holy, self-forgiving process with each burden. Remember to embrace the block, to be open to the Divine Wisdom Gift contained within it, to be guided to that place within you that needs your unconditional love and acceptance. Then take each block to the purifying fire of your heart and FORGIVE YOURSELF with these words: "I bless myself. I love myself. I forgive myself." As the flames of your heart engulf the block you repeat to yourself: "I allow the Love of God within me to consume this burden, and the power I have given it. And I am Free. Thank you God." [*Pause* . . . .]

Your process of Self FORGIVENESS ends with the last burden block smoldering in the purifying fires of your own Heart. Your whole being seems now to reflect the Love and Light of your Holy Self. The lightness and love that you feel now are indescribable. Your heart space is fully illuminated and you realize that your forgiveness work has opened your heart to radiate out its compassionate light to your body, and to the entire energy field surrounding you. It feels as if your body is enveloped in a cocoon of soft and pristine white light filled with love and self-acceptance. As you bask in that love, know that you are now a pure, clear, unburdened channel for the Love of God.

Your Holy Self beams joy and peace to you as you float out of your loving heart embraced by its light. Knowing that you are always with your Holy Self, you return your consciousness to your physical body and find it illuminated with the Light and Peace of God. Feeling unbounded gratitude for this journey of Self FORGIVENESS, you emerge from it feeling Whole and Complete, aware that you have surrendered to the Light of God, the Divine Presence within you.

ACKNOWLEDGE YOURSELF

Giving the GIFT of FREEDOM
Through Self FORGIVENESS to You!

You are free. . . . Celebrate! Call your Prosperity Prayer Partner and plan a special outing together. The work you have done individually can be acknowledged together with a special dinner, a rock concert, a good movie, a sports event, or a visit to an art exhibit you have been wanting to see. Let your creativity soar in planning this freedom party together. You deserve it. Acknowledge yourself for consenting to receive this GIFT of Self FORGIVENESS and allow yourself to feel your freedom—freedom to live an Abundant Life!

CHAPTER 7

TITHING

Give Back

Threlease you experienced through giving the GIFT of FOR-GIVENESS to others and to yourself has left you feeling buoyant, lighthearted and full of joy. The mysterious Gift-Giver has certainly given your soul presents that are already changing your consciousness . . . and you know that they are changing your life! You can't wait to open the next GIFT.

There are only two left. The one wrapped in white paper printed with different denominations of money peaks your curiosity. You grab it and begin to open it with great anticipation.

It turns out to be the "T" of GIFTS—TITHING. As you unwrap the green and white paper you find a parchment scroll inside. It is titled "The Mechanics of TITHING." Uh-oh. Suddenly the lightheartedness in your chest turns as heavy as that last rep at the very end of your workout. "What does this have to do with living an Abundant Life?" you ask.

I want to take a moment here to prepare you for this GIFT. When you read the word TITHING, did you notice a wisp of fear, a slight feeling of disgust or shame, or even a little bit of mind boggle? Well, know that you're in good company if you did! That "T" word seems to pack a wallop every time, be it by inducing unpleasant mental states or the opposite ones of joy, feeling in the flow, or eager willingness to give.

My personal reaction to the concept of TITHING was pure avoidance. When confronted with the idea that TITHING was related to my ability to live a prosperous life, I just couldn't or wouldn't accept it. I actually skipped the chapter on TITHING that was included in the first inspirational book on prosperity I read. The very mention of the word triggered a strong, unhappy memory from my childhood. I was brought back to my seven, eight, nine and 10-year-old self watching my parents' behavior immediately preceding and following the annual home visit from our parish priest. It was not a pleasant sight! The bickering, fear and depression I saw coming from them around those visits was palpable. At those ages, I did not understand what went on during that yearly closed-door meeting. I just knew that I dreaded this annual event because it left a sooty black cloud hanging over our household for weeks that I simply didn't understand.

I later came to realize that the express purpose of that visit by the priest had not been to check on our welfare but to solicit my parents' tithe for the coming year. It's no surprise that I came to associate TITHING with those disturbing memories and unconsciously used that connection to build my loathing of the word itself, never mind the actual practice. It has only been through a great deal of prayer and practice that I have come to realize the immense importance of this GIFT of TITHING. More than that, I have come to find out that by **not** tithing I was dooming myself to a life of poverty and lack. For in reality, the resistance to TITHING is empowering an erroneous belief that there is not enough.

What is TITHING? It is the spiritual practice of giving. It is practicing the privilege of being a divine circulator—the receiver and the giver—of the gifts of God. TITHING means giving back to your spiritual Source 10 percent of all you have been given. When we pay God first, we are consistently affirming God as our Source and the Supplier of all we receive.

The word *TITHE* means *tenth*. The practice of tithing was originally observed by giving one tenth of one's crop or flock to the source of one's spiritual support such as a church or clergy. Tithing was practiced by virtually every civilization over the course of history, including the great empires of Babylon, Arabia, Persia, Egypt, China, Greece and Rome. Tithing is the principle underlying even the ritual of sacrifice practiced by indigenous cultures. According to Dr. Ponder, the ancient people felt that *ten* was the "magic number of increase."

— In her powerful book, *The Dynamic Laws of Prosperity*, Dr. Catherine Ponder explores the relationship between prosperity and TITHING. She writes, "True prosperity has a spiritual basis." She goes on to say that your talents, abilities, yes even your mind and body are channels of your prosperity. However she claims, "God is the Source. Therefore, you must do something definite and consistent to keep in touch with that rich Source, if you want to be consistently prospered."

In modern times, our incomes have replaced the crops and produce of old. What remains the same is that God is the Source of all that we receive. So it is that all avenues of our monetary income form the basis for TITHING. We must apply the 10 percent to that total.

Now, if you are having difficulty swallowing at this point, let me offer a glimpse of the glorious big picture that we are literally standing in, perhaps unaware. TITHING of money is a practice that opens us up to live abundantly in *all areas* of our lives, not just financially. Through TITHING we align ourselves with the universal abundance of God, thus allowing ourselves to receive more of the gifts available from the Unlimited Source of Wealth. By TITHING 10 percent of **all** our income on a consistent and regular basis, we can live in the *expectancy* of being prosperous in all areas of our lives. We can expect increases in our well-being, relationships, and creative self-expression, as well as our finances.

For the most part, the whole concept of TITHING has been presented to us as a one-way practice: the obligation of the tither that benefits the recipient of the TITHE (i.e., the church, synagogue, mosque or clergy). In other words, we were taught that, through our sacrifice and giving, the church would prosper, e.g., the parish could expand, the school could have more supplies, the new building could become a reality more quickly. Rarely were the benefits to the giver presented.

So what **is** the benefit to the tither? Imagine for a moment that you have a rich aunt/uncle in the invisible realm whose greatest and only desire is to give you everything your heart longs for. Imagine that it's this being's great and good pleasure to give to you. Imagine that the only block to your receiving all that you can possibly want—and more—is your willingness to open your heart and soul to accepting more. Then imagine you are blessed with a formula that, when followed, will act as the key to that opening. That key is to give back a portion of what you are receiving to this invisible relative.

Imagine that, as you learn to keep 90 percent of what you have been given, what you have kept expands—that you can literally watch the 90 percent go further than the original whole amount. And what's more, by leaving 10 percent of what you have been given, you have sent a clear message to your rich aunt/uncle, "I am open and receptive to more of your generosity." This scenario, in essence, is the Law of Circulation in motion. *The giver is God and the receiver is you.* The giver to God's storehouse (the person or place from which you have received your spiritual nourishment) is you and the receiver is God. And so it goes. You are in the flow . . . expressing the Abundance of God that is your true nature and you are reaping the rewards from being a tither.

More than a little curious as to what you can do with this fourth GIFT, you pick up the parchment scroll titled "The Mechanics of Tithing." You run your fingers through the soft satin bow of silver and gold. You untie it and begin to peruse the instructions for giving this GIFT.

THE MECHANICS OF TITHING

WHO TITHES? You do! If you are in a relationship and your partner is not willing to TITHE, it is important for you to identify your portion of income and TITHE on that. A conversation with your significant other on this subject may well be one of the richest ones you'll ever have.

HOW MUCH DO YOU TITHE? 10 percent from **all** sources of income! You give on the gross if you're employed, on the net (after business expenses) if you're self-employed. Please be aware of the trap many fall into by thinking that the salary from your job, draw from your business, and interest from your trust or pension are the only sources by which you are supplied. This is not true! The Infinite Giver is sourcing you in infinite ways, if you were just to become aware of them. TITHING is the practice that raises your awareness of how wonderfully supplied you are from many, many streams. TITHING is done on all sources of income including what we refer to as "unearned" and "unexpected," such as trusts, benefits, profit sharing, inheritance, alimony, interest, dividends, and even tax refunds. Tax refunds? Yes, even tax refunds, because they too are in-come. When you have committed to the practice of TITHING you have tapped into the true joy of giving from an overflow of abundance!

Be open and be aware! If you ever have a question as to whether it is appropriate to TITHE on some supply you have been given, check into the Mind of your Heart and listen to its reassuring voice. Guided from that place, you will know what to do. It is very important to remember the metaphysical principle: **You Can't Outgive God!**

NOTE: Giving 2 percent is not tithing. It is giving or sharing, but we cannot call it "tithing" because it does not allow you to be a full participant in the Law of Circulation. Remember,

TITHE means one-tenth. If you are working your way up to 10 percent, please do not call your practice TITHING until you are giving at least 10 percent of all income to God's storehouse.

TO WHOM OR WHAT DO YOU TITHE? To the place from which you receive your spiritual nourishment! Where is it you have felt the voice of God speak to you, the hand of God reach out to you, the presence of God remind you of who you are? Your church, synagogue, mosque, spiritual practitioner? Favorite inspirational author or teacher? The neighbor who just happened to say a word of wisdom that changed your life? By being very conscious of the Presence of God, you can give your TITHE to that person or place that is representing God's Love and Wisdom in your life. (Note: In general, charitable giving to your favorite cause is **not** TITHING. To support a non-profit organization, such as The American Cancer Society, your local PBS station or the Boy Scouts, is a wonderful gesture, but all donations should be considered over and above the practice of TITHING.)

HOW OFTEN DO YOU TITHE? Consistently! **Pay God First** as soon as you receive your income. Your goal is to joyfully anticipate your first opportunity to TITHE on what you have been given. If you are paid weekly, TITHE weekly. If you are paid monthly, TITHE monthly or apportion your tithe and make a weekly contribution if that is more comfortable for you. The most important thing is to write your TITHE checks first, knowing that the 90 percent left expands to meet all of your needs and more.

WHAT IS YOUR ATTITUDE? One of Joy! You commit to TITHE freely and gratefully and lovingly, from a place of over-flowing abundance. This may take practice until you really feel it. As is common with the initiation of any new practice, you may experience the temptation to dissolve into the ego fears of there not being enough. Step over the temptation and give.

Your goal is to refrain from any sense of "bargaining with God." Giving with expectations of what you will get in return is destructive to TITHING and to living an Abundant Life. By freely giving from a consciousness of *expectancy* rather than the mental attitude of expectation ("I'll give and then I'll get") you can relax into knowing that all of your needs are met because you are in the flow of Divine Circulation.

WHAT RESULTS CAN YOU EXPECT? You are in the flow of Life! Tithers have issued the following delightful alerts:

- Be prepared to witness your 90 percent expand.
- Be prepared to see your bills paid, your income increase, and your fears dissolve.
- Be prepared to experience a new sense of serenity when it comes to money, bills and job-related hassles.
- Be prepared to experience a story similar to this one: After he had been TITHING for several months, George happened upon a website that listed unclaimed property. Much to his surprise he discovered an account that had belonged to his deceased grandfather, to which he now had legal claim. Suddenly, he found himself the beneficiary of thousands of dollars. He couldn't wait to write out his TITHE check.
- Above all, be prepared to be fully aligned with the Divine Giver whose love and generosity knows no bounds. By giving the GIFT of TITHING, we acknowledge the Truth: All of Life is a Gift.

A Mystic Speaks on Tithing

Joel S. Goldsmith
from *The Art of Spiritual Healing*

Supply is one of the easiest demonstrations that a spiritual student can make, but there is a vast difference between the spiritual truth about supply and the human sense of it. In spiritual truth, supply is not income; it is outgo. To the human sense, the reverse of that is true. Spiritually, however, there is no way to demonstrate supply. It cannot be done because all the supply that exists in heaven or on earth exists within you at this moment, and therefore, all attempts to demonstrate supply must result in failure. There is no supply outside of your being. If you want to enjoy the abundance of supply, you must open out a way for that supply to escape. . . . Because of the infinite nature of your being, you cannot add health to yourself or wealth or opportunity or companionship: All you can do is to recognize that you embody all that God is and has. You must not try to get; you must not try to have; you must not try to draw to you; you must learn how to let Infinity flow out from you. . . . Scripture has given us this teaching (of giving) under the name of tithing, that is, the giving of one tenth of one's income to God.

Personal Success Story

A Real Life Moment Of
TITHING

The Power of Tithing
by Donna Jacobs

I had heard about tithing when I was growing up but believed it was an exclusively Protestant religious practice. I grew up Catholic and, though we were expected to contribute generously to the church, tithing per se was not talked about.

The concept of tithing entered my life when I began attending a Religious Science church in early 1990. Although I did not participate in that way, my awareness was being heightened through the principles I was learning. After taking some classes and joining the church, I was invited to fill a term on the board of trustees by someone who was stepping down. One of the requirements of board membership was to tithe to the church. That was a real stretch for me since I was divorced and living on much less income than I had been accustomed to in my marriage. I did it anyway, holding my breath, and I trusted that it would all work out.

Little did I know that there would be many blessings that would come to me. My faith grew stronger and deeper and my life became richer. I found that I really had no less discretionary income when tithing than when I wasn't. I was amazed. My life continued to become better and better.

I felt led to move to California and made the move in August 2000. By this time I had been a prayer practitioner for four years and was planning to go to the school of ministry. When I arrived in California I was filled with enthusiasm, confidence and passion to create a new life for myself. My plan was to get a job, find a place to live, and then enroll in school. I attended church regularly and was always a generous contributor, but I stopped tithing at that time using the rationalization that I would begin to tithe again when I had a job, my own home, and a "home" church.

It took six months to find a job—much longer than I had thought it would. A month after I started work the company decided to downsize. As the "new kid on the block" I was the first to go. I began to get depressed. Then, after working hard to get my real estate license, I tried to get started in that field. By now it was spring of 2002. I decided that I was going to return to Ohio if I wasn't in a position to have my own home by that fall.

I enrolled in Rev. Diane Harmony's class, *5 GIFTS for an Abundant Life!*™ And it changed my life! I made the commitment to tithe once again . . . and this was scary with so little income to my name. My life began to change. The day after I signed the agreement with myself to tithe I received a check in the mail for $20,000. Half of it was to be mine and half was to be given to some other people. My immediate thought was that I wished this had come before I signed that agreement! I sure could use the money after not working for two years and having my unemployment run out.

I swallowed hard and wrote out that tithe check for $1000. And then money began coming to me from many places. The check I had been waiting for from the moving company to cover damages arrived. One of my brothers put money in my hand when I saw him, telling me that more was on the way. And it was. He sent me a monthly check for $100 to help me through my financial slump. There were other monetary gifts, but the abundance was showing up everywhere for me.

As I worked through the process in class I began to get clarity about my life. As a result of my childhood experiences, I had spent a lifetime believing that I wasn't wanted. I had done therapy around that issue and felt peaceful about my childhood but I still carried that feeling of not being wanted or loved. I saw my great nephew the weekend that my brother put the money in my hand. We had a fantastic time together and he showered me with love and affection. I drove home from our visit in tears with the realization that I am loved and wanted. That child taught me of my value and I was open to receive it as a result of the *5 GIFTS* course. I was able to remember that I am important and my life serves a purpose.

I had been judging myself so harshly that I eroded any belief I had in myself. It became clear to me that my path was to return to Ohio no matter what the circumstances were in my life by the end of the summer. Events took place that made it clear that my place was there and that I was to return "home" even earlier than I had originally planned. All that . . . and more . . . was restored when I finally said "Yes" to God again by giving 10 percent of my income to my source of spiritual nourishment.

The story continues. I found a job two weeks after my return to Ohio. A month later I signed a contract on a house and am now living in my very own home again with all my possessions that had been in storage for two years. I've learned to appreciate so much during this time and am continually grateful for each moment of my life. I have been able to detach from "things." And although it is wonderful to be in my own space with my own things, I've learned that they are not what matters in life. My spiritual connection is what I value most and tithing keeps me ever aware of God showing up in all areas of my life. I stay in the flow by being part of the flow! That's the way it works. I will NEVER allow myself to block my good by closing down to the joy of tithing.

I have just finished facilitating the first *5 GIFTS for an Abundant Life!*™ course to be given in Ohio and I am joyous to see transformation take place in the lives of those who attended. One person believes my journey to California and back was to allow her to receive what she did from the class. Her life has changed as well. People blossomed and bloomed, and we know that the growth will only continue. What a blessing it is to be in the flow of life! It's just like surfing, so ride the wave. . . . We are continually supported and all is provided. All we have to do is say "Yes."

Kicking and Screaming All the Way
by Tina Fox

If there is anybody on this earth who has fought tooth and nail against the idea of tithing, I guess that would be me. It wasn't for lack of trying—for months on end I would try to tithe. I would carefully figure out 10 percent of my net income—to the penny—and then I would panic at giving away what seemed like such an enormous sum of money. I would grit my teeth as I wrote the check and as soon as I gave the money to the "source of my spiritual food" for that month, I would suddenly find myself just this side of destitution. The money in my checkbook would disappear before my eyes! I'd sit with my bills all around me, wondering where on earth the money had gone and then I would pause, shake my head and mutter, "Tithing . . . yeah, right! Just look at how well tithing works—I'm broke! Tithing is supposed to unleash the abundance of God into my life—what happened?" So I would stop tithing. As soon as I stopped tithing, I would feel a tremendous sense of relief and money would immediately flow back into my life. Of course, with so much more money in my life, I would feel guilty about not tithing and so I would try again. I would tithe and the money and resources in my life would dry up within days. As soon as I stopped, the money would flow back in. It did not take too many repetitions of this pattern before I came to the conclusion that tithing obviously wasn't working for me.

One day I decided on an impulse to start "giving." There were people in my life who were such blessings to me and I felt this urge to give something back to them. I decided that if I felt moved to give, then I would give. I did not think about how much I was giving and I did not think about getting anything back in return. I gave because I was so thankful to have them in my life and so grateful for the gifts they had given me. Within a very short period of time I found that I was giving far in excess of 10 percent of my gross income, and yet I seemed to have more money than ever before. It seemed like the more I gave, the more I had. There was always more than enough. Eventually, it occurred to me that I *was* tithing—tithing in the truest sense of the word.

When Rev. Diane speaks about tithing, she frequently refers to "giving from the overflow." When I was trying so hard before, I was giving from a sense of obligation, or fear, or with the hopes of getting something back—I was giving from a position of profound lack. I really had nothing to give in that moment and the universe was kind enough to point this out to me by halting the flow of resources in my life. When I started giving from the overflow of my love and appreciation for the people and gifts in my life (without any strings attached), then I was really "giving" from the limitless capacity of God within me—and the universe responded in kind. It's been about four years now since I adopted this "giving" practice. As long as I give from the overflow of abundance, love, and thanksgiving in my life, there is always more than enough.

Give Your Gift PRACTICE

Heart Opening Instructions
for
TITHING

Now is the time for you to call your Prosperity Prayer Partner and arrange a time to meet. Be sure to bring along the following contract. Once together, you can begin your TITHING session in prayer. From that prayed-in place, you can read aloud your "Contract With God." Proceed to sign the contract and bear witness to your Prosperity Prayer Partner's contract. Vow to one another that you will be there to support each other at least once a week through the fears, tears, joy and abundance that this commitment carries. Discuss with one another ideas about where you will be tithing for the next ten weeks. (Remember, according to the ancients the number ten is the "magic number of increase.") End the session in prayer and begin the sacred, spiritual practice of TITHING.

CONTRACT WITH GOD
MY HOLY AGREEMENT

Being fully aware
that I AM an infinitely prosperous emanation of God,
and that God is my one and only Source of all Supply,
*I do now pledge to tithe 10 percent of **all** my income for the next*
ten weeks to the person or place from which I am receiving
my spiritual nourishment.
In holding the Truth that tithing is a spiritual practice,
I willingly, joyfully and gratefully give to God first.
I commit myself to change my consciousness to knowing that
I AM Prosperous,
for I realize and claim that my changed consciousness
leads me to a more abundant life.
I enter into this agreement surrendering any belief in separation
from my Source, My God, my Abundant and Prosperous Self.

_____   _____
Your Name   Prosperity Prayer Partner's Name

Tithing Dates for Ten Weeks beginning _____ and
ending _____.

ACKNOWLEDGE YOURSELF

Giving the GIFT of TITHING
to You!

Make a commitment to live *in expectancy* of receiving unplanned income. When it arrives—and it will—as a direct result of your TITHING, plan to take a portion of it to spend on yourself. Keep your Mind of the Heart Map close at hand and be ready to fund one of your INTENTIONS from the abundance you are activating through TITHING.

CHAPTER 8

SURRENDER

Give Over

Awave of sadness rolls over you as your gaze falls upon the last of these amazing GIFTS delivered by the Giver of the secrets to living an Abundant Life. By now, you are truly enjoying your simple yet profound practice of acknowledging in your GRATITUDE Journal five gifts of each day that you are especially grateful for. You are honoring yourself at ever-deeper levels by setting your INTENTIONS clearly and meaningfully and allowing them to manifest with grace and ease. You are experiencing the sweet blessings of life renewal through the practices of Self FORGIVENESS and FORGIVENESS of Others, and you are centered in your commitment to TITHE 10 percent of all of your income in recognition of God as your Source. Your life has indeed become richer, and you are a true receiver and giver of these amazing GIFTS. "What else is there?" you ask.

Then you remember that you set out on this journey of discovery not just to have abundance but to be the Abundance of God! And while you're not sure what that really means, based on your experience up to this point you have every reason to believe that this last GIFT must be at least as powerful as the first four.

With the kind of anticipation that's eager and reluctant all at the same time you now reach for the last present. It is long, thin, and very flat, like a 12-inch ruler, and its tag reads:

SURRENDER!
Through giving this GIFT you allow the Good of God into your Life!

You open the iridescent wrapping to find a long book mark inscribed with an affirmation that is written in bold black letters:

I SURRENDER TO THE POWER AND PRESENCE OF GOD WITHIN ME

That's powerful! . . . But what about that word "surrender"? You're not sure you like the sound of that one at all. And some years ago I would have heartily agreed, because that word has the ability to provoke shudders that ripple through the ego mind. Let's go to the Webster's Collegiate Dictionary to make sure that our egos are not shuddering in vain. Here's one of the definitions of the word: "give oneself up to another's power or control." Common synonyms for *surrender* are relinquish, yield, submit and resign. There certainly doesn't seem to be any kind of a promise of an Abundant Life in these words with their connotations of defeat and powerlessness.

When asked what the word *surrender* means to us, most of us answer with words like "resignation," "giving up," "lethargy," "I don't care any more," and "You win, I lose." The image of a white flag waving on a battlefield may come to mind . . . the war is over, and, if we are on the side behind the billowing white sheet, we are bloodied, defeated, and facing our fate of being either captured or killed. Not a positive or pretty image to be sure!

But at this stage in our GIFTS journey we know that the mysterious Stranger would not deliver a GIFT that would be so antithetical to the promise of an Abundant Life. So now what are we to think? . . . Perhaps the key to distinguishing SURRENDER from its human/ego definitions and understanding its GIFT is to look at *to whom* we are being asked to surrender. And the answer is right there on the affirmation card: *to the Power and Presence of God Within*. Ahhh . . . now that concept might just unlock the door to SURRENDER as the powerful spiritual practice that it is!

When we let go and let God, we are in the midst of a spiritual practice so powerful that the core beliefs that have held us captive and small can be dismantled, resistance to our good can melt away, fear of the unknown can be shattered, a sense of oneness with God and all life can be embodied, and a whole new world of infinite possibilities can open up for us.

And to what or whom do we practice the act and art of SURRENDER in order to experience these beautiful, abundant benefits? Not to something or someone outside of ourselves as required by the non-spiritual concept of SURRENDER, but to the God *within* us. It is deep, inner work to SURRENDER the ego/little self to the Divine Self that is the very core of us. It is through realizing that this is an "inside job"—that the real issue has nothing to do with giving up to an authority in our outer world or accepting defeat in any way—that we are empowered.

"Thy Will (not mine) be done," when truly embraced, will create the opening for Spirit to reveal a realm of choices and opportunities impossible for us to know from our small, defended, ego-driven selves. Here are a few testimonials from 5 GIFTS students:

- "By releasing the illusory idea that I control life, I free myself to select from a multiplied number of choices which the universe offers."
- "While I used to view surrender as an act of giving up, I now perceive it as an act of giving over."
- "It is a conscious choice to allow the power and presence of God to live Its life as me."

Imagine *allowing* the sweet Divine Presence within to live your life! Imagine the choices open to you then. Imagine the ease and grace of each moment of each day. Imagine the relief you would feel if you really knew that you are not alone . . . that you do not have to do it all yourself . . . and that within you is a *knower*, guiding you, directing you, maintaining you and sustaining you.

Imagine surrendering into that Wise, Holy Self. That is sweet SURRENDER.

When we SURRENDER to the Power and Presence of God Within, the synonyms for SURRENDER take on a whole new meaning.

- *Yield:* to yield to the flow of life rather than oppose it.
- *Relinquish:* to let go of resistance to accepting what is, to allow ourselves to choose differently.
- *Resign:* to reassign our little selves to the service of our Holy Selves and to the guidance S/He offers. We are resigning ourselves to *more* of the Goodness of God.
- *Submit:* to submit our will to the Divine Will of God within us. We are submitting our inner ear to listening to the Still Small Voice that is forever offering Its inspiration to us.

In the words of a 5 GIFTS graduate, "Be sure to render it all to God . . . Sure to Render . . . Surrender."

When we give the GIFT of SURRENDER, it expresses itself in our lives as the quality of Trust. Usually we are called on to SURRENDER our way of believing and/or doing things when we are out of options and have nowhere else to turn. When the pain is too great, when what we've thought would work fails time after time, and when the resistance to change is so strong that our bodies are stiff and tight and our emotions are beyond frazzled, we find ourselves with no other choice than to give up and turn it over. To make that choice is to be at the headwaters of the River of Trust. Surrendering to the Power and Presence of God Within allows us to float freely on the wisdom of the Holy Self, guided by the internal voice of Intuition and powered by the winds of the Love of God, to the shores of infinite possibility.

I SURRENDER TO THE POWER AND PRESENCE OF GOD WITHIN ME!

A Mystic Speaks on Surrender

Eckhart Tolle
from *The Power of Now*

I f you find your life situation unsatisfactory or even intolerable, it is only by surrendering first that you can break the unconscious resistance pattern that perpetuates that situation.

Surrender is perfectly compatible with taking action, initiating change or achieving goals. But in the surrendered state a totally different energy, a different quality, flows into your doing. Surrender reconnects you with the source-energy of Being, and if your doing is infused with Being, it becomes a joyful celebration of life energy that takes you more deeply into the Now. Through nonresistance, the quality of your consciousness and, therefore, the quality of whatever you are doing or creating is enhanced immeasurably. The results will then look after themselves and reflect that quality. . .

It is the quality of your consciousness at this moment that is the main determinant of what kind of future you will experience, so to surrender is the most important thing you can do to bring about positive change. Any action you take is secondary. No truly positive action can arise out of an unsurrendered state of consciousness.

Personal Success Story

A Real Life Moment Of
SURRENDER

Surrender

by Catherine Espinoza

I view the act of surrender as returning to my faith that Spirit is in charge—letting go and letting God. In this activity of release I must also know that God is inherently good, and that the unfoldment of Its blessings is always in right timing and for my highest good.

Usually I choose to surrender when life is becoming too much for me: it is overwhelming; there is too much to do; I am struggling; situations are overly challenging; life is not cooperating with my expectations. When I allow myself to consciously take a breath, to step back from the circumstances and go within, I often discover that I have stepped into that spiraling ego ride that always moves in a downward fashion. I am plummeting into the abyss of "me-ness." It is *me* that has too much to do. It is *me* that is working too hard. It is *me* that is giving too much. It is *me* that isn't being valued. It is *me* that believes she has to do everything herself.

As I learn to recognize this pattern within myself I know that I can choose differently. I can step back into that place of higher consciousness, that place of remembering the Truth of Life: that God is all there is, and that it is God's great pleasure to give us the Kingdom. What I embrace in the evolutionary process of life and consciousness is our consistent residence in that sweet, uncertain place of surrender, each of us simply being the absolute faith of Spirit's expression as all facets of our life.

For a long while I have found myself puzzling over the famous scene in *The Wizard Of Oz* in which the Wicked Witch of the West writes across the sky with exhaust from her broomstick the words "Surrender Dorothy." For many years I thought it meant that the witch was demanding that Dorothy give herself and the ruby slippers up to her. Because this cryptic message was written in the sky above the Emerald City of Oz where all the inhabitants could see it (and in particular the wizard himself), I also have considered that the witch could have been telling Oz to surrender or to give Dorothy up into her clutches.

Using a more spiritual interpretation, could it be possible that the witch was, inadvertently or subconsciously, helping Dorothy step into that powerful place of faith by reminding her to surrender or "let go and let God"? Because of the witch's skywriting Dorothy was able to get through the doors to have an audience with the wizard, receive an answer to her request, destroy the witch, and aid her friends in getting their desires granted. It was the power of Love and Caring—of mind, heart, and courage (or spirit)—that enabled Dorothy to finally find her way home.

Perhaps each of us has that "witch" inside who revs us up to forget that we are expressions of God and then, in the end, has the wherewithal to remind us of the Truth of our being by asking us to surrender to the infinite goodness and Divine Right Action of Spirit. With Spirit there is always a way. Now, if I can just remember where I parked my broomstick. . . .

Give Your Gift PRACTICE

Heart Opening Instructions
for
SURRENDER

TRUST AND SURRENDER EXERCISE

This exercise is designed to allow you to feel in your mind and your body the spiritual practice of SURRENDER.

Call your Prosperity Prayer Partner and make a date to do this simple assignment together. Stand about two to three feet in front of your partner with your back to your partner. Your partner's job is to catch you under your arms as you hold your arms out from your sides, stiffen your body like a board and fall back into your partner's arms. Each time you do this be aware of how it feels to Trust and Surrender. Notice the shift that occurs when you allow yourself to let go completely—you will know when that happens. At that point, you are ready to switch places with your partner and allow him/her to have this amazingly simple yet profound experience of Trust and Surrender.

A GUIDED MEDITATION: Releasing Resistance

(To be read to you by another or recorded in your voice for you to listen to. Do not read or record the words in brackets [ ]. These are "stage directions.")

Gently close your eyes and bring your attention inward. Let go of any attachment to the outer world as you focus on your breathing. Take a deep breath in through your nose. . . . Inhale. . . . Fill your lungs to capacity, and then hold it. Open your mouth slightly

. . . and . . . exhale very slowly. . . . The more slowly you exhale, the more your body will relax . . . unwind . . . slow down. . . . Very good.

Inhaling once again . . . take a deep breath. . . . Fill your lungs completely . . . and hold it. Open your mouth slightly and EXHALE very . . . slowly. Enjoying the feeling of letting your body unwind . . . relax . . . let go. That's right. . . .

Inhaling once again . . . this time imagine the Light of God filling your entire being . . . bringing a sense of peace and relaxation to every part of your body from the top of your head . . . down to the tips of your toes. . . . Good.

Now, let your breathing return to its natural rhythm . . . and put your attention gently on it, as you continue to relax your body . . . and let go . . . breathing easily and effortlessly. . . .

As your body continues to relax . . . turn your attention to your mind. Release any connection to the thoughts you find there, and allow it to become empty . . . and relaxed as well. [*Pause* . . . .] . . . And now focus your attention on your heart space. Let your heart open as you continue to feel the deep sense of relaxation wash over your body . . . your mind . . . and your heart. [*Pause* . . . .]

And now . . . become aware of your emotional body, noticing any feelings that might be surfacing in this space of deep relaxation. It is in the emotional level that we hold on to the beliefs and patterns that keep us in the place of resistance . . . and in the clutches of non-surrender into the Higher / Holy Self . . . where in all our possibilities lie. Resistance lives in opposing the new . . . opposing change. It takes the form of a clenched fist wrapping its hand around our minds and bodies . . . the fear of letting go. . . . It hides in the thoughts of hanging on . . . in the emotions of not letting go. And it lodges in our bodies as stress and tension and clutching and clinging. . . .

Scan your emotional self now. . . . Sense and feel any feeling of resistance to a situation or idea that is calling you to surrender . . . to change. . . . [*Pause* . . . .] . . . Invite that feeling to come into your awareness . . . into a space of non-resistance that embraces it without judgment or fear. . . . [*Pause* . . . .] . . . Notice where it is showing up in your body. . . . Is it lodged in one particular area of your physical form? Can you feel tightness in your shoulders, perhaps? Your solar plexus? Around your heart? . . . [*Pause* . . . .] . . . Where is your tongue in your mouth? Pressed up? Curled down? Up against your lower teeth? Notice how your body is responding to the resistance you are feeling . . . working to shut down the discomfort found there . . . to expel it by resisting it. . . .

Watch how the mind clenches against the unwanted idea of letting go, of changing . . . of becoming more of Who You Are. . . . See it struggle to distract . . . to argue . . . to ignore. . . .

And now, bring your attention to your heart space . . . the place where Spirit lives within you . . . the place of Sweet Surrender into your Holy Self. Enter that space and feel the feelings of peace, harmony and tranquility found there . . . the feeling of Oneness with all of life. . . . From that safe and loving harbor of your heart, invite your mind to gently open . . . to respond to your full acceptance of its struggle to hang on. . . . Invite in the pain and suffering that are caused by the action of resistance. . . . Invite it all to soften . . . the edges all around the thoughts of holding on . . . the fist of resistance releasing its grip, loosening and letting go. . . . [*Pause* . . . .]

As the fist of your mind opens its fingers . . . opening . . . opening . . . releasing . . . releasing . . . you feel the surrender of your thoughts directly affecting your emotions . . . and your physical being. As you allow the sensations and feelings of your emotional self to surface . . . in an atmosphere of acceptance and love

... there is a moment to moment letting go of the resistance, the tension ... the pain ... a melting of the clutching and clenching feelings ... tensions dissolving into the softness. The edges melting into the warm embrace of Acceptance, Love and Compassion ... softness ... floating ... free ... the sensations dissolving into space ... into the nothingness from which they came ... dissolving ... releasing. Resistance is melted away in the warmth of your heart ... [*Pause* ....] ... Resistance to pain ... to the unknown ... to discomfort ... even to surrender—feel it now in the melting of all tension from your body temple ... the body softening and relaxing and melting away all tightness ... stress ... and holding on. ...

[*Pause* ....] ... The body is soft, the mind is open ... soft and open. Sensations that arise are dissolving, neutralizing, floating free in the soft body ... the open mind ... moment to moment surrender ... moment to moment letting go into your heart space ... into that vast opening of God within you ... moment to moment Love and the Light of the Divine melting any residue of resistance ... letting go into the heart of your being ... letting go into the arms of your Holy Self ... beyond the body ... beyond the mind ... resting fully into your heart space ... into the Heart of God.

And when you're ready you can slowly and lovingly bring your awareness back to the present moment. ... Become aware of your body here and now ... [*Pause* ....] ... Gently open your eyes ... feeling free and fully surrendered into the heart of God ... into your Holy Self.

ACKNOWLEDGE YOURSELF

Giving the GIFT of SURRENDER
to You!

Give yourself the GIFT of further releasing resistance from your body temple. Sit in a sauna or relax in a hot tub under the stars. Take a long, relaxing bath. Call today to make an appointment for a massage, an herbal wrap, a facial, or a pedicure. Sign up for a yoga class. Or give yourself the luxury of extending your daily meditation practice by ten minutes. You deserve it!

CHAPTER 9

YOUR ABUNDANT LIFE!

Give Glory

The packages left by the mysterious Stranger have all been unwrapped. Yet the GIFTS remain etched in your consciousness, in the Mind of your Heart. You are becoming skilled in the practices of giving the GIFTS of GRATITUDE, Setting and Manifesting INTENTIONS, FORGIVENESS of Self and Others, TITHING and SURRENDER. It appears that by giving these GIFTS to yourself and to others you are activating your birthday wish to live an Abundant Life.

Your life is changing—like the speed of sound in some areas of your life, and seemingly slowly and subtly in others. You are probably beginning to identify with any number of people whose stories you have read or heard, people who have experienced transformation in their lives from giving these 5 GIFTS. You now have your own to share. This would be a perfect time to call your Prosperity Prayer Partner to say "Thank you." What a wonderful journey you have shared together! Make a date to get together to look at your Mind of the Heart Maps once again. Acknowledge yourselves for traveling this path together and create a ceremony to celebrate *being* the Abundance of God. Perhaps you might build an altar together, using symbols that represent Abundance and Prosperity to you. Give the GIFT of Glory to the Divine by joining together in prayer once again.

Perhaps you have felt a shift in your attitude toward your financial circumstances since beginning to give your GIFTS. Maybe you didn't win the lottery as you had been hoping when you began to read this book. Maybe you find yourself at about the same level of income that you had when you started this journey, but you have become aware that even after giving 10 percent to the place or person that represents God's presence in your life, you have enough to meet your needs. And perhaps your reaction to your current circumstances is less volatile and less stressed than it was before. It is from this place then that you SURRENDER into being that wide-open channel for God's Abundance and Opulence to flow into your life.

You may notice that your job is a nicer place to be these days now that you have given the GIFT of GRATITUDE for the little things—like the flavored coffee in the cafeteria or the soothing color of your workspace. With your career INTENTIONS from the Mind of your Heart Map firmly rooted in your awareness, perhaps you're not feeling as confined in your current employment because you truly can see that it is an essential steppingstone to realizing your dream. You know you are *doing* and *detaching*. . . . You know that all is well!

Are your relationships a little smoother? . . . Do you find you are giving and receiving a little more harmony and compassion with family members, co-workers, a lover and/or friends? If so, you are experiencing the natural effect of giving the 5 GIFTS, especially the Gift of FORGIVENESS. Even as it impacts all areas of our lives, FORGIVENESS can most profoundly enrich our lives in the arena of relationship. If you have not noticed any change yet, check inwardly—do you feel a little stirring to set the INTENTION that a certain relationship become more harmonious? Or perhaps you want to add that "ray" to the Relationship Life Dimension of your Mind of the Heart Map.

Have you noticed any change in your health and well-being . . . do you have more energy . . . a desire to eat foods that are more nourishing? Do you have a greater willingness to let go of habits and addictions that no longer serve you? Do you find you no longer need to depend on medications to swing your mood or relieve aches and pains? Are you finding that you are listening to your body and what it wants . . . that you are honoring it when it says "rest," "exercise," "fresh food," "bedtime"? Living juicy through prayer—knowing that you are the Wholeness and Perfection of Spirit—may have been at work here. Self-care and self-love are natural results of receiving and giving the 5 GIFTS.

Have you had any "faster than the speed of sound" experiences yet? Has $10,000 or more come in the mail after you wrote your first TITHING check, as it did for one of my students? As a result of prayer with your Prosperity Prayer Partner, have you started a new business that is taking off like a rocket? Has a diagnosis of cancer proven to be a false alarm? Has the long-awaited wedding taken place? Has your divorce become final with both of you remaining friends? Do you have the itinerary in hand for your dream pilgrimage to Egypt? Have you received the phone call "out of the blue" from the relative you'd not spoken to in years? Have you finally had a good night's sleep after releasing the all-consuming anger, fear and resentment you'd been holding toward your addicted teenager? Has someone accepted your proposal . . . agreed to publish your book . . . bought your product in quantities beyond your wildest hopes . . . given you the audition . . . named you as heir to a small fortune . . . promoted you . . . proposed to you . . . realized that you are the love of his/her life? Every one of these *changes of circumstance* has happened in the very real lives of my 5 GIFTS students.

AS YOU GIVE THE 5 GIFTS, SO SHALL YOU RECEIVE!

And so you are to be commended for the work you have done, the results you have seen. With some sense that "this stuff works," you breathe a sigh of deeper SURRENDER into the God Presence within you and drift into a meditative silence. Taking comfort in the manifestations that have occurred for you (whether large or small), you allow your attention to drift inward with each inhalation and exhalation. As you go within you are feeling whole and complete, in a way you've never fully experienced before.

You draw in your breath easily and deeply, and you become aware of what a rich experience this is, this simple act of breathing . . . its rhythm so calming, so peaceful. You notice how your awareness naturally finds its way home, home to the Mind of your Heart, that now familiar place where you feel so welcome and so safe. Relaxing there, floating on the softness of your breath, to your wonder and surprise you feel that sense of a familiar Presence. Can it really be? Yes . . . it is the mysterious Stranger! And you have no sooner realized this than your awareness opens to the recognition that this Bountiful Stranger . . . is You. Your Divine Self is the giver of your 5 GIFTS for an Abundant Life!

*Without the need for words, you enter into a deep conversation with this Being of Wisdom and Light, the very source of these amazing GIFTS for your soul. You are made aware once again that the GIFTS you have received are meant for so much more than manipulating the material world. You are reminded that the demonstrations of health and wealth in all areas of your life are simply a by-product of the true purpose of giving these GIFTS . . . the true purpose, you now understand, is always to remind you that you are a Divine Circulator of **all** of the GIFTS that are God. Feeling totally in harmony with this Loving Being, you respond to Its thoughts in full agreement that your only purpose is to reveal the True Nature of God in every moment of your life. You are an instrument of God, and you are here to allow Spirit to play Its holy melody through you. You are free to feel more deeply the spiritual awakening to the Truth that you **are** the Abundant Love of God.*

Immersed in the awareness of your Oneness in God, you are invited by the luminous figure to open your inner eyes to the vision set before you. Your attention is captivated by the wondrous sight that is unfolding. It is

142

a brilliant view of the Earth from outer space . . . an Earth that is a planet of plenty, a place of peace, a landscape of love. Hardly recognizable for its lack of turbulence, war, famine and borders, you become aware that there are no "haves" and "have-nots" in this scene. There is no one in survival mode, going hungry, sick without care, needing money or desperately seeking a job. And there are no boundaries. In this picture, there is no fighting over "mine" and "yours" for all have an abundance of what they need and every desire is fulfilled.

Looking even more closely, you notice that this verdant globe is abounding in opulence of every kind—plants, animals, sumptuous foods, wonderful shelters, and clothing for all seasons in plentiful supply. All of the inhabitants are lifted out of lack consciousness and are sharing the richness of this place by being in service to one another . . . freely giving their GIFTS. And perhaps most wondrous of all, as each person is living the Abundance of God, all are free to recognize that Truth in others! And so you gaze upon a world of human beings fully expressed as God beings.

In what can only be described as your deepest soul recognition of the collective spiritual longing of all sentient beings, you stand in holy awe and breathe in the full picture of the impact on the planet when each soul is spiritually awakened to its highest calling. You now catch the meaning that the mysterious Stranger, your Divine Self, wants you to understand by showing you this scenario. By giving the 5 GIFTS for an Abundant Life, you are witnessing the planetary possibility of your spiritual awakening multiplied by millions and millions. You have been gifted with the vision of our planet populated by souls living on purpose . . . being the Abundant Love of God. You are witnessing Heaven on Earth!

PRAYER &
MEDITATION

The daily practices of prayer and meditation are meant to bring you into conscious communion with God. When you are actively engaged in either of these, you are communicating with the Divine that is within you and all around you.

Each of these Keys to the Kingdom allows you to perfect the art of *speaking* to God (prayer) or *listening* to God (meditation). In either case, you are treating your soul to a journey home to its origins, and you are bringing yourself into full alignment with the Truth of your being. When practiced on a daily basis, you will open yourself up to a dimension of your life that will eventually be embraced as the wellspring from which all else flows.

Prayer

Many of us have learned some form of communication with God. For the most part, most of us have learned to pray to a God that is outside of ourselves. The tone of that prayer has usually been one of supplication or beseeching. For our purposes here, when asked to initiate a daily practice of prayer during this journey to a Consciousness of Wealth, I suggest that you put that form of praying aside and "try on" the idea of affirmative prayer. That is, after recognizing that there is but one God and that you are an expression of The One, state that you **know** that what you are praying about or for is **already** yours. Then, you can give thanks that what you desire is already manifested, and let go and let God.

Your daily prayer time might include a prayer along these lines:

There is only one Power in the Universe and I name it God. The God that is within the stars, moon, sun and all of human-hood, is within me. Realizing that all that God has is mine, I know that my body is whole, vital, healthy and well.

I am grateful that I am the wellness of the Divine. I release this prayer and know that it is so. Amen.

In this simple format, you have affirmed the Truth of your being.

Meditation

There have been reams written about the power and enormous rewards reaped from having a daily practice of meditation. I have listed a few references for you below. For our purposes, I strongly recommend that you adhere to a daily 15 to 30 minute "inner time in the Divine" (preferably in the morning upon arising), in order to witness the thoughts that are running around in your mind. By taking this time to become consciously aware of the contents of your consciousness, you also can become aware that you are not those thoughts, but you are the Thinker.

As the Thinker, you have dominion over where you choose to put your attention—whether in the meditative time, or in your waking world. As you take this time in the silence, the thoughts in your mind might not settle down, but you will hone the power to behold them and to remain still, listening with that inner ear for the Still Small Voice that is forever whispering, "You are my Beloved, in whom I am well pleased."

If you are a beginner, I recommend that you practice the stillness by sitting in a comfortable place where your back can be straight. Uncross arms and legs (unless you prefer to be on the floor with legs in a lotus position). Place your hands in your lap with palms up or down, depending on what's comfortable for you. Close your eyes and focus your attention on your breathing. Watch the breath as you naturally inhale and exhale through your nose. Be the observer. If your attention wanders off with a thought, gently—without judgment—bring it back to your breath. Practice this for 15 to 30 minutes a day and witness the subtle changes you experience in your life.

Meditation breeds detachment and stress reduction. It trains you to hear the Voice of God that can be heard in the space between your thoughts.

Reference Books on Meditation

Journey of Awakening: A Meditator's Guidebook by Ram Dass

How to Meditate: The Acclaimed Guide to Self-Discovery by Lawrence LeShan

In addition, there is a plethora of audiotapes, retreat centers and weekly meditation sittings offered throughout the world.

Chapter Notes

CHAPTER 2:
Christian D. Larson, *The Pathway of Roses*. (Lakewood, CA: Mannahouse Publishing, 1993), p. 236.

CHAPTER 3:
From *Science of The Mind* by Ernest Holmes, copyright 1938 by Ernest Holmes. Copyright © renewed 1966 by William M. Lynn. Used by permission of Jeremy P. Tarcher, an imprint of Penguin Group (USA) Inc., p. 194–195.

CHAPTER 4:
Alan Cohen, *A Deep Breath of Life*. (Carlsbad, CA: Hay House, Inc., 1996), Apr. 18.

From the book *The Seven Spiritual Laws of Success* © 1994, Deepak Chopra. Reprinted by permission of Amber-Allen Publishing, Inc. P.O. Box 6657, San Rafael, CA 94903. All rights reserved., p. 88.

Christian D. Larson, *The Pathway of Roses*. (Lakewood, CA: Mannahouse Publishing, 1993), p. 245–247.

CHAPTER 5:
Meredith L. Young-Sowers, *Angelic Messenger Cards*. (Walpole, NH: Stillpoint Publishing, 1993), p. 90. Text has been excerpted with written permission from Stillpoint Publishing.

CHAPTER 6:
Paul Ferrini, *The Twelve Steps of Forgiveness*. (Greenfield, MA: Heartways Press, 1991), p. 14.

CHAPTER 7:
Joel S. Goldsmith, *The Art of Spiritual Healing*. Copyright © 1959 by Joel S. Goldsmith. Reprinted by permission of HarperCollins Publishers Inc., p. 142, 143, 145.

Catherine Ponder, *The Dynamic Laws of Prosperity.* (Camarillo, CA: DeVorss & Company, 1985), p. 175.

CHAPTER 8:

Eckhart Tolle, *The Power of Now.* Copyright © 1999. Used with permission from New World Library, Novato, CA 94949, p. 173–174. *www.newworldlibrary.com*

About the Author

IANE HARMONY is the founder of Universal Harmony Inc., an organization dedicated to empowering the planet's population with the spiritual insight, knowledge and tools to live life in abundance, joy and peace. She is a compelling and compassionate speaker, teacher, author, licensed spiritual counselor and ordained minister of a trans-denominational philosophy. The proud mother of 5, Diane is blessed with a true gift of communicating her wisdom gained through years of personal growth and spiritual self-development. Her search for a personal Consciousness of Wealth led her to create a transformational course upon which this book is based. Diane has licensed facilitators around the globe to teach *5 GIFTS for an Abundant Life!*™ courses. Hundreds of people so far have been transformed by taking these classes. In addition to the 5 GIFTS course and book, Diane has recorded numerous audio tapes and CDs and has given hundreds of talks on the subjects of *Gratitude, Intentions, Forgiveness, Tithing* and *Surrender.* She is as comfortable speaking to thousands of people at a conference as she is in an intimate classroom situation. Diane's passion for her vision, her integrity in walking her talk and her compassionate heart are the strengths she brings to all her work.

Diane lives in Southern California on a bluff overlooking the Pacific. When not spending time with her children and grandchildren, Diane can be found leading groups to sacred places like Hawaii to swim with the dolphins.

Gifts you have received from giving the 5 GIFTS

If you have a story about how you practiced the spiritual principles described in this book to create a Consciousness of Wealth in some area(s) of your life, and would like to have your experience considered for inclusion in a future book, please submit it to the address or email below.

www.5GIFTS.com
5 GIFTS for an Abundant Life
2658 Del Mar Heights Rd. # 199
Del Mar, CA 92014

Give the gift of
5 GIFTS *for an Abundant Life*
To Your Friends, Family and Colleagues

❑ YES, Please send me_____copies of *5 GIFTS for an Abundant Life* $15.95 each.

❑ YES, Pease send me _____copies of the companion *5 GIFTS for an Abundant Life* CD containing the two guided meditations transcribed in the book, "Releasing Resistance" and "Self Forgiveness" recorded by Diane Harmony for $13.95 each.

❑ YES, I am interested in having Diane Harmony speak and/or give a seminar to my organization. Please send me information.

❑ YES, I am interested in hosting and/or attending a *5 GIFTS for an Abundant Life!*™ course.

❑ YES, I want to be on your mailing list to be notified of future events, seminars and retreats.

QUANTITY	ITEM	PRICE	TOTAL
_____	_____	_____	$_____
_____	_____	_____	$_____
_____	_____	_____	$_____
	1st Book or CD Shipping & Handling		$7.95
	($1.50 for each additional item)		$_____
	Sales Tax (CA residents add 7.75% sales tax)		$_____
	TOTAL ORDER		$_____

Payment must accompany all orders.

My check or money order for $_____is enclosed.

Please charge my ❑ Visa ❑ MasterCard

Name _____

Address _____

City/State/Zip _____

Phone _____ E-Mail_____

Card# _____ Exp. Date _____

Signature _____

Buy on Online at www.5GIFTS.com

BY PHONE: (800) 955-7452

BY FAX: (858) 350-4557 Fill out and send this form

BY MAIL: Mail completed form along with your remittance to:

Universal Harmony House

2685 Del Mar Heights Rd. #199 • Del Mar, CA 92014